THE CHAPEL OF THE THORN: A DRAMATIC POEM

By
Charles Williams

Edited and introduced by Sørina Higgins
with a Preface by Grevel Lindop
and an Essay by David Llewellyn Dodds

apocryphile press
BERKELEY, CA

Apocryphile Press
1700 Shattuck Ave #81
Berkeley, CA 94709
www.apocryphile.org

CHAPEL OF THE THORN Copyright © 2014 The Estate of Charles Williams.

The preface is an adapted extract from *Charles Williams: The Last Magician* by Grevel Lindop, Oxford University Press, 2015. Copyright © Grevel Lindop 2015; used by permission.

The appended article by David Llewellyn Dodds was first published in the *Inklings-Jahrbuch 5* (1987). Copyright © David Llewellyn Dodds 1987; used by permission.

Printed in the United States of America
ISBN 9781940671536

Table of Contents

Preface (Grevel Lindop) 1

Introduction (Sørina Higgins) 5

The Chapel of the Thorn 39

Notes 107

Appendix (David Llewellyn Dodds) 123

Bibliography 141

About the Author 145

About the Editor 147

Preface[1]

CHARLES WILLIAMS is remembered, amongst other achievements, for having written novels concerned with the Holy Grail, the Philosophers' Stone, and the Tarot. But he was not the only member of his family with an interest in objects of mystical significance. In 1910, his uncle Charles Wall (an author, artist, and archaeologist of High Church views) published *Relics of the Passion*: an illustrated book surveying the various objects that had been venerated in the middle ages in churches and shrines across Europe as genuine items used in the martyrdom of Christ. These included supposed pieces of wood from the True Cross, nails used in the crucifixion, fragments of Christ's garment, vessels containing His blood, and of course the famous Turin Shroud. Wall also briefly summarized the legends of the Holy Grail (Wall 152-3),[2] though, as no church has claimed to possess the Grail itself, it could not be discussed as a "relic." The category that received the longest treatment was that of thorns purporting to be from the original Crown of Thorns. Wall was able to list no fewer than fifty-six places that displayed individual thorns or the entire crown.

Relics of the Passion must have stirred Williams's imagination, for on November 6th, 1911, he was offering to send his mentor, the poet and critic Alice Meynell, "the scheme of a dramatic poem dealing with the clash of the ecclesiastical and the mystical (permit the word!) *not* of the Reformation period, but somewhere about 900 A.D." The play—probably meant for reading, not performance—would be called *The Chapel of the Thorn*, and the "clash" it depicted would be the struggle over possession of a thorn from Christ's crown and the chapel where it was housed. Whether or not Meynell saw the outline, Williams finished his play the following summer, dating the manuscript "Augt. 24 / 12." He must have completed it as soon as he had dealt with the complexities of getting his sonnet sequence *The Silver Stair* (Herbert and Daniel, 1912) through the press. He lent a copy of the play to Alice Meynell in the summer of 1914 (as recorded in a letter from Meynell to Williams on July 10th of that year), and certainly hoped for her critical opinion and advice; but though she kept it until May 1915 and promised to discuss it with him, there is no evidence that she ever did so.

There is in fact a real "Chapel of the Thorn": Santa Maria della Spina, at Pisa. Ruskin was fond of it, and mentions it several times in his writings (for instance, *Works* 358, 419). It was duly listed by Wall. But Williams's play takes place in an unidentified place—merely a chapel between a road and a sea-cliff—at an unspecified time in the middle ages. The "chapel" of the title is the shrine of a sacred thorn, a relic of Christ's crown, guarded by a solitary priest, Joachim, and his young acolyte, Michael. The play depicts a three-cornered struggle among mysticism, represented by Joachim; the Church, represented by the local Abbot, Innocent; and paganism, in the form of Amael, a bard and high priest of the Old Gods. Abbot Innocent plans to extend the abbey wall to enclose the chapel and take away the thorn so that its prestige and pilgrims will be drawn to his abbey. Joachim is determined to keep the thorn at his humble chapel and has the local villagers' promise that they will, if necessary, fight to keep it. What he does not know is that the village men are concerned only because the chapel has been built over the tomb of Druhild, a pagan hero who (it is said) will one day rise from the dead (II:186-89). For their Christianity is only superficial: whilst the womenfolk venerate the Virgin Mary for her healing powers, the men are pagan to the core, clinging tenaciously not only to their myths of Druhild "Of the night and Of the Trees" (I:40; see also the note on I:135), but also to their traditional custom of buying young women to keep, alongside their wives, as concubines or "chamber-maids" (I:15, I:21, II:394).

The play consists largely of debates, with a few skirmishes that hardly come to blows, among the three viewpoints of the mystic, the ecclesiastic, and the pagan bard. Joachim sees the Church as a mere cynical agent of exploitation (I:835-43), and believes that following the Church's rules is pointless. Only direct spiritual experience has any value (I:844, 847-52).

Abbot Innocent argues that the way of the mystic, with its trust in love and freedom, is too demanding for ordinary people. For their own good, they need authority and rules (I:861-67, 879-81). The Abbot acknowledges Joachim's holiness and, even, speaking to the Prior, calls him "a greater man than we" (I:998); but in the name of the Church he is ready to use force to seize the chapel and take away the thorn. His position gains some support when we hear a local villager, arguing with the Abbot, justify the trade in women by quoting garbled fragments of Joachim's mystical teachings, "that by love and the desire of man / Toward woman" he can "find out God" (II:236-37, 234). The Abbot squashes this plea firmly: "It may not be… This is an ill thing" (II:241, 44). It is a fascinating passage. Williams is showing up an obvious misunderstanding of his own, and Coventry Patmore's, assertion of the mystical connections between erotic love and spiritual experience—connections which Williams would later explore more fully in *Outlines of Romantic Theology*. At the same time, this debate over the enslavement of women knowingly reflects Alice Meynell's feminism, and she was doubtless expected to approve. But one suspects that it also touches, ambivalently, on a private fantasy of Williams's own.

Contrasted with both the Abbot and Joachim is Amael, pagan priest and bard, who is paying a final clandestine visit to the region before taking ship for distant lands. Amael is defiant in his scorn for Christ, the Church, and the timid ways they impose on men. He represents a heroic, pagan, and brutal world, and he is given much of the play's best poetry. He admits that he has performed human sacrifice twice (I:706-08). But he can also be modest, calling himself "a little dust / Blown from the ruined temples of the gods" (I:612-13).

And he has a good line in anti-Christian irony. When the Abbot loses his temper, Amael exclaims: "O the white cheeks of your Christ. / They can be red with anger then? His mouth / Perchance is dumb with fury, not with fear?" (I:697-99). Amael's most important dialogue is with Michael, Joachim's young acolyte. Joachim fondly imagines that, provided the Thorn can be retained, Michael will one day take his place at the chapel as its priest. But Michael has become bored and restless. He longs for a life of adventure, and his heart is stirred by Amael's tales. Amael urges him to leave the tame life of the chapel and sail with him as his pupil to learn magic, poetry and the harp (II:125-45). Amael also claims to have journeyed, shaman-like, to the source of the energies of life:

> I have gone down and in a dark night laid
> My hands upon the leash of that desire
> Which evermore the gods let loose on us,
> And felt about my brows the wind-like lust
> That blows to changing shapes this mist of men! (II:286-90).

In the play's second and final act, the tensions among Church, inner spiritual life, and paganism remain unresolved. They cannot be resolved because, clearly, Charles Williams sympathizes with all three viewpoints. One might say that intellectually he acknowledges the case for the Church's authority; that his heart is with the mysticism of Joachim; but that he responds viscerally to the pagan glitter of Amael's world. The energies and tensions that will form his major poetry are coiling and struggling in *The Chapel of the Thorn*, and the play's debate is Williams's own inner drama. Taliessin, the harp-playing bard of the late poems, is already visible in Amael; and in Taliessin's world too women will be bought and sold.

The play also shows us that certain magical or esoteric ideas had already made an impression on Williams. On the very first page of the play, the protecting pentagram, later an important image, makes its unexpected *début*. Williams had probably encountered the "five-cornered shape" of the pentagram, as a protection against evil spirits, in the pages of Eliphas Levi's *Mysteries of Magic* (190). And when Joachim sadly foresees that Michael will leave him to follow Amael, he seems to envisage some form of reincarnation, or at least a prolonged post-mortem spiritual pilgrimage (II:553-61). This concept suggests Eastern ideas about vast cycles of lives, perhaps filtered through Theosophy or the like.

There are also traces of the views set out in A. E. Waite's *Hidden Church of the Holy Graal*. Arguing with the Abbot, Joachim tells him that disciples of the official Church are like strangers who come to the porch of king's house and find that "within the king hath poured the wine" (I:901). In contrast to the Abbot's external rites, Joachim has "beheld the Holy Bride, the Church, / Caught to her mystic marriage through the world, / Wed to her Lover in all mortal things" (I:927-29). These passages seem to reflect Waite's argument that there is "a priesthood within the priesthood, a Mass behind the Mass" (Waite 621), a "more secret place which lies behind the sanctuary of the Visible Church (620), and that despite "absolute belief in the truth of doctrinal Christianity, …behind all doctrine there was something great and undemonstrable, the direct knowledge which had departed because the world was unworthy" (636). For Joachim, as for Waite, the true church—the room where the king pours out the wine—is in the experience of the mystics. The visible Church, though its teachings and sacraments are valid, is merely a useful shell, an outer porch to the true sanctuary.

For all its occasional clumsiness and naivety, *The Chapel of the Thorn* is a vigorous work that shows rich poetic and dramatic talent. It seems odd that Alice Meynell showed so little interest in it. Did she find the play in some way disturbing? Did it perhaps suggest a danger that her protégé Charles Williams, like the acolyte Michael, might break away from the path set out for him by his elders and betters? We shall never know. But in retrospect, *The Chapel of the Thorn* acquires a quite different aspect; for we can see it as a prelude to his major Arthurian poetry, in which he would once again, and much more powerfully, evoke the Britain of the "Dark Ages" with its rich blend of pagan and Christian, the magical, the mythical and the spiritual. A little over a century after its composition, it is a delight to see this rich and fascinating early work in print at last.

—Grevel Lindop

---

[1] This preface is an adapted extract from *Charles Williams, The Last Magician* by Grevel Lindop, Oxford University Press, 2015. Copyright © Grevel Lindop 2015; used by permission.

[2] Please refer to the bibliography at the end of this volume for all works cited in the preface, introduction, and appendix.

INTRODUCTION

In the archives of the Marion E. Wade Center in Wheaton, Illinois, rests a little century-old notebook. The title page reads:

THE CHAPEL OF THE THORN:
A DRAMATIC POEM

This short play in verse is one of the earliest works written by Charles Williams (1886-1945): poet, novelist, editor, teacher, Christian, occult master, and member of the Inklings with C. S. Lewis and J. R. R. Tolkien. In this tightly-woven, two-act poetic drama, priests contend for control of the crown of thorns: a relic preserved in honor of Christ's crucifixion. Meanwhile, as Christians fight among themselves to determine who should have custody of this sacred object, adherents of a quasi-druidic religion clamor for access to the same site, because their hero lies buried beneath the Chapel. Tensions rise and battle is threatened, but syncretism and ambiguity leave the conflict open-ended.

Many tensions are operative in this short play: Christian vs. pagan religions, sacred vs. secular political power, and debates over the justice of the proposed war. Such conflicts could be read as a tale for the early 21st century as well as the early 20th. In addition to its applicability, the spiritual perspective lends the work a timeless quality, as it does in all of Williams's best work. Although there are lively debates between characters—voices raised, fists shaken, executions threatened, and battles looming—the most profound changes occur inside individual souls. Throughout Williams's writing, every external attitude or action has a theological dimension: he portrays the natural as interpenetrated by the supernatural. In many of his books, resolution is achieved by the subordination of the person to the symbol, the piece to the pattern, and the soul to God.

Williams had a systematizing mind, and myth and ritual were among the most important structures on which he built symbolic constructs. He attempted to fit every idea, person, and event into the elaborate mythology that he constructed out of Christian theology, Rosicrucian hermeticism, and Arthurian legend. This is true in his writing and somewhat illuminated by his life. Some among his acquaintances felt that he played a part, casting them in roles rather than seeing them as individuals, and that he wore a mask hiding his real nature. Lang-Sims argues that his "personality was interiorised to such an extent that nothing in [his] outward environment reflected it by so much as a hint" (Lang-Sims 19). It is only fair to contrast this perspective with others who believed that "in every circle that he entered, he gave the whole man" (Lewis, *Essays* v). Both views should be compared with W. H. Auden, who found himself in Williams's company to be "in the presence of personal sanctity," and who "felt transformed into a person who was incapable of doing or thinking anything base or unloving."[1] Others (who may not have known of the hermetic rituals) claimed that "the man himself had an immediate charm and likeability, a radiation of benevolence and amiability," that "he was somehow protected from evil, and was himself a protection," and that "I have never known a healthier-minded man than Williams" (Eliot xi, xiii-xiv, xv). These quotes paint a picture full of contradiction. An exploration of his biography further complicates the matter. Is synthesis achieved in his writing, or do the paradoxes raised by his life echo throughout his works?

BIOGRAPHY

Charles Williams, poet and metaphysician, was born in north London on September 20th, 1886.[2] He spent most of his life in London and was a city man by habit and imagination. The City figures prominently in his writings and in his theological ideas as an embodiment of order and authority. He found another important manifestation of order, hierarchy, and fellowship in the Oxford University Press, for which he worked from 1908 until his death. During his nine-year courtship of Florence Conway, he began to develop one of his distinctive concepts: a Theology of Romantic Love, which was his courageous attempt to apply the *Via Affirmativa* to love and sex. He nicknamed Florence "Michal" after King David's unappreciative wife, because she scolded him for quoting poetry loudly in public. In spite of a volume of verse (*The Silver Stair*, 1912) debating the merits of practicing celibacy and renunciation as steps along the *Via Negativa*, Charles and Florence finally married in 1917.

That same momentous year, he also joined a secret society: the Salvator Mundi Temple of the Fellowship of the Rosy Cross.[3] This was A. E. Waite's Christian mystical offshoot of the Order of the Golden Dawn. Williams remained a member of this occult society for at least ten years, climbing rapidly up the grades and serving as Master of the Temple for two six-month periods. Its imagery and "ingenious construction of arbitrary relationships between different symbolical systems" (Howe, qtd. in Morrisson 32) are essential to his writing.

During the 1920s and 30s, Williams worked for the Press, wrote incessantly (including six of his seven metaphysical novels), taught evening courses through the City Literary Institute, and carried on an intense but unconsummated affair with the Press librarian, Phyllis Jones (whom he called "Celia"). He also entered into a "master-disciple relationship" with several young women, subordinating them to roles in his personal mythology and utilizing them in rituals designed to stimulate his creativity (see Newman 2, 5; Lang-Sims 17; and Hadfield *Exploration* 106).

In 1939, the London offices of the Press were evacuated to Oxford due to the Blitz. There, Williams joined "The Inklings," the group of Christian writers including C. S. Lewis, J. R. R. Tolkien, and Owen Barfield. He also began lecturing at Oxford University and was granted an honorary M. A. in 1943. Williams's most important work is from this last phase of his life, including the great Arthurian poetry (*Taliessin through Logres*, 1938, and *The Region of the Summer Stars*, 1944), his most powerful dramatic work (*The House of the Octopus*, 1945), a final novel (*All Hallow's Eve*, 1945), and his synthesis of theology and literary criticism (*The Figure of Beatrice*, 1943). In these last works Williams expressed another of his characteristic concepts: the idea of Substitution or Exchange, in which people can carry one another's emotional, spiritual, or medical burdens as literally as carrying a box or bag for someone else. Williams died in Oxford on May 15th, 1945, just one week after victory had been declared in Europe.

THE CHAPEL OF THE THORN

Charles Williams thought of himself as a poet from a very early age and had already chosen his life's subject matter by 1912, the year of *The Chapel of the Thorn*. The Arthurian legend was the myth onto which he patterned his literary work, his personal life, and his interactions with family members, friends, and coworkers. This little play, with its dramatization of spiritual tension and mythic ritual, is a good starting point for an examination of his peculiar theology and literary accomplishments.

The Chapel of the Thorn is one of Williams's earliest works. He seems to have dabbled in the development of verse drama before this; see, for instance, the juvenile *Prince Rudolph of Silvania* manuscript fragments,[4] written for "domestic consumption only" (Hadfield *Introduction* 19-20). His family engaged in amateur theatricals at home, so drama was in his ear and his imagination from a very young age. Yet *The Chapel of the Thorn* appears to have been the first dramatic work that he completed and considered suitable for publication. It did not find a publisher in its time. Of course, Williams was also writing poetry from an early age, and published his first volume of verse, *The Silver Stair*, in 1912, the same year as the completion of *Chapel*.

MANUSCRIPT HISTORY

The manuscript held in the Marion E. Wade Center in Wheaton, Illinois (CW / MS-39), is a gem of Edwardian culture. It rests in the archives, tenderly cared for yet rarely read. When I signed out the original notebook in Williams's elegant handwriting on June 8th, 2012, I was the first to handle these cream-colored, pre-war pages (besides the archivists) since Raymond Hunt deposited them there in 1973; other researchers have worked from a photocopy. A few other scholars have read it, but the text had never before been transcribed.

Inside the archival folder is a small bound blank book, 7.81" (20.10 cm) high, 6.00" (15.20 cm) wide, and 0.50" (1.35 cm) deep. The binding has mostly come off so that the stitching is visible. The cover is missing. Several of the sections are loose and falling out. The pages are very slightly yellowed. A tidy, thin handwriting, carefully centered and neatly aligned, politely offers lines of verse without crowding the sheets. Wide margins surround the poetry, which is set up for performance with the name of the character preceding each speech. The lines of dialogue are carefully parallel. Charles Williams wrote only on the right-hand pages. His friend and office-mate Frederick Page wrote on a few of the blank left-hand pages, offering comments, suggestions for revision, and observations about the action. There are one hundred and thirty-eight sheets of paper in the research photocopy, which reproduces all the right-hand pages Williams wrote on and only those left-hand pages on which Fred Page jotted notes. Williams himself used and numbered one hundred and five pages in the notebook.

The chronology of the manuscript is a bit vexed, especially as there appear to have been two copies circulating at various points between 1912 and 1973. For those who revel in facts and dates, here are the particulars as they are currently known.[5]

1911. Grevel Lindop reports[6] that on November 6th, 1911, Williams wrote to Alice Meynell, offering to send her "the scheme of a dramatic poem dealing with the clash of the ecclesiastical and the mystical (permit the word!) *not* of the Reformation period, but somewhere about 900 A.D." As will become clear below, the finished play has a less determinate historical setting—but this quote does suggest that Williams was beginning to plan out the plot of *Chapel* in the autumn of 1911.

1912. Williams finished *The Chapel of the Thorn* on Aug. 24th, 1912.[7] This manuscript is very clean, neat, and legible, which may suggest that it is a fair copy rather than the rough sheets on which he originally worked out his ideas. This, then, may mean that Aug. 24th was the date he finished copying it out, not the date on which he completed composing it. Williams then gave this clean manuscript to his colleague Fred Page for comment. Page wrote remarks on the blank left-hand backs of the sheets, then returned the notebook to Williams.

Williams took many of Page's suggestions into account, writing neat emendations over or beside the original lines. As these changes are sometimes in pen, sometimes in pencil, it is clear that Williams went over the text twice, making changes as he went. The fair-copy is in pen, and Williams initially edited the text, marking sections and changing words in pen either as he was copying it or soon thereafter. Then Page critiqued the MS in pencil. Many of these suggestions were left as Page made them, written into the MS (which occasionally leads to confusion: does Williams leave a comment unremarked because he wants to use it, or because he does not want to use it?). Then Williams went on to make further corrections after receiving the MS back from Page. This later stage of editing is somewhat confounded with Page's suggestions, because Williams's later editing was also done in pencil.[8]

Williams's responses to Page are usually minor line edits, but are sometimes more drastic, including the deletion of passages and little side-conversations in the margins. It is pleasant to observe the documentary evidence of a friendship and to know that Williams was not intractable when it came to revision.

This all occurred before Williams sent the play to anyone else.

1924. According to Alice Mary Hadfield (Williams's co-worker and quasi-biographer), Williams attempted to get *Chapel* published sometime in 1924—that is, she records his remarks about being disappointed that no one liked the play. While she does not explicitly state that he sent it out to publishers, the excerpts she quotes from his letters at this time seem to suggest that he did, probably to Oxford University Press, where he worked.

If Williams did send *Chapel* out to be considered by publishers in 1924, which copy was it? Did Williams make (or have made) another copy, either a manuscript or a typescript? His usual practice was to have his works typed. Or did this same manuscript (Wade CW/MS-39) travel from Williams to Fred Page, then back to Williams, then to the publisher, then back to Williams, and then onwards? It appears to me to be too clean, too little handled, for that to have happened. Perhaps a forensics specialist needs to be called in to take fingerprints.

In any case, after rejecting *Chapel*, the publishers must have returned their copy (whichever one it was) to Williams, for he sent it to another friend, John Pellow—or else he sent a typescript to the publishers, who kept it, and Williams sent the handwritten copy to Pellow. Here are Hadfield's remarks:

> He finished a play[9] and sent it to John [Pellow] on 10 May 1924 saying 'nobody loves it (except me)', asking for his opinion on the theology rather than the verse. He tried to turn the manuscript from a two-act into a one-act piece and messed it up. Is this, perhaps, the lost *Chapel of the Thorn?* (Hadfield *Exploration* 39).

Thankfully, Hadfield is wrong on this point, and the play is not lost.

Williams continued to mourn the rejection of his work and to suffer setbacks, as his *Outlines of Romantic Theology* was turned down by Oxford University Press. He wrote again to Pellow on September 6th, 1924, saying: "So the unfortunate *Romantic Theology* shall cuddle the equally unfortunate *Chapel of the Thorn* in a private seclusion" (Hadfield 45). Just as *Outlines of Romantic Theology* found a publisher after Williams's death,[10] so *Chapel* has happily done the same.

1925. John Pellow transcribed some passages from the play on July 3rd, 1925. Pellow later gave these selections to Hadfield. She does not note when he did so, but suggests that this occurred after Williams's death. Neither does she give any hint about what Pellow did with his copy of the entire play: whether he kept it, gave it away, destroyed it, or returned it to Williams.

1926. Williams's disappointments continued, for Faber's rejected two novels: *The Corpse* and *The Black Bastard*. Williams again complained to Pellow in May of 1926 about these rejected works: they "can all go away with *The Chapel of the Thorn*" (Hadfield 45-6). Fortunately for posterity, these were later published by Victor Gollancz with revised titles: *The Corpse* in 1930 as *War in Heaven* and *The Black Bastard* in 1933 as *Shadows of Ecstasy*.

1942. Sometime in the thirty years between 1912 and 1942, Williams sent that original fair copy from August 24th, 1912, to another friend: Margaret Douglas. On April 1st, 1942, Douglas mailed it to Williams's student, disciple, and would-be Boswell, Raymond Hunt.[11]

1973. Raymond Hunt donated his "revised authorial holograph" (the same one from back in 1912) to the Marion E. Wade Center. This is the copy from which I worked and apparently the only one still extant.

1983. Hadfield further notes that she possesses what she thinks are the only extant pages from *Chapel*—extracts that appear to have been lost:

> John Pellow gave me eight pages of extracts which he had made from *The Chapel of the Thorn*. He said that the work was early and pseudo-Miltonic in style. 'Re-reading it for the first time after many years I experience some of the admiration which prompted me to go to the trouble of copying patches of it.' These pages in my possession are all that seem to remain of the work" (Hadfield *Exploration* 238 n. 10).

We can be thankful that Hadfield was wrong in this case.

To summarize: It appears to me that there must have been two copies of *The Chapel of the Thorn* extant in 1924: (a) Williams's manuscript from 1912; and (b) another version that he sent to publishers in 1924.

Williams fair-copied (a) from his notes or working draft in 1912 and sent it to Fred Page for comment. Page returned it to Williams who revised it and sent it to Margaret Douglas. She sent it to Raymond Hunt, who ultimately donated it the Wade where I transcribed it.

Copy (b) could have been either a manuscript or a typescript. It is possible that it was a later, revised, version of the text presented in this edition. It was probably sent to publishers in 1924, rejected, and returned to Williams. He may have sent it to John Pellow, who made eight pages of extracts that he sent to Hadfield. We do not know what became of the original. Hadfield only knew of the existence of one copy, which she thought had been destroyed, and therefore she concluded that the play no longer existed.

Only one exists now, as far as I have been able to determine. Pellow's extracts have disappeared. No one has been able to trace another copy. There is no copy in the Bodleian library. There is no copy in the library of the Charles Williams Society. We can be thankful there is one copy in the Wade.

Plot Summary

The Chapel of the Thorn appears to be set in Britain during its period of provincial loyalty to Rome or soon thereafter—i.e., somewhere between the third and fifth centuries A.D. The main action of this short drama occurs just outside the Chapel where the Crown of Thorns is kept.

As a side note, there is some discussion among readers of this play about whether the relic is a single thorn, a strand from the Crown, or the entire Crown. It is frequently called "The Thorn" in the text of the poem (as well in the title, of course). There are a few references that seem to refer to the whole Crown, such as Innocent's demand in I:994: "Wilt thou yield up to me this Crown of Thorn" and the stage direction at II:619, which directs Innocent to turn, "*lifting up the Crown.*" Gregory says that "it was about the white Christ's brows / When he was slain" (I:101-02). There are several possibilities. Williams might be leaving these references intentionally ambiguous, not wanting to burden the reader with a history of this relic (which was, interestingly, traced by his uncle Charles Wall in a book entitled *Relics of the Passion*, 1910) nor get his poem entangled with debates over the location or condition of the true crown. Or it is possible that Williams had read his uncle's book and concluded that "Joachim, Innocent, et al. are competing for a fake relic once foisted upon this St. Cyprian" (Dodds, "Re: Concerning the relevant relic"). Finally, he could be suggesting that this relic is at least part of the original true crown. But like other ambiguities in this play, he leaves the question open.

Whatever this relic may be, it is central to the action. Several people are vying for control of it or for occupation of the site of the Chapel: Joachim, Priest of the Chapel of the Holy Thorn; Innocent, Abbot of the nearby Monastery of St. Cyprian; King Constantine; and Amael, a singer and pagan priest of a quasi-Druidical religion. The villagers are caught up in the conflict of their leaders, as well. Some characters want to keep the Crown of Thorns where it is, some to build a wall around it, some to move it to the abbey for safe-keeping, and some to return the Chapel to a place of pagan worship. The Thorn reveals each person's spiritual condition by their responses to it and their subsequent treatment of each other.

Thus the conflict is more complex than a simple two-way debate between Christians, some of whom who want to keep the Thorn where it is and others who want to move it to another location. The local pagans also venerate the spot where the Chapel stands. They go so far as attending Christian services and participating in all Catholic rites—because their heroic semi-divine figure, Druhild of the Trees, is buried right under the Chapel. These pagans first express a willingness to fight against Abbot and King to preserve the Chapel in its place; later, however, they withdraw their support. In other words, these pagans participate in external Christian worship, but remain faithful to Druhild in their hearts; a rather complex devotional choice, perhaps, and certainly a daring plot device on Williams's part.

Not much happens by way of exterior action throughout the play's two acts. The drama is nearly all spiritual, as characters find their true natures revealed through their responses to the Thorn and the dispute.

The epigraph of the play points to a key theme: "Think not that I am come to send peace on earth: I come not to send peace but a sword. . . a man's foes shall be they of his own household" (Matt. 10:34, 36). Although it is true that there are other conflicts besides quarrels among Christians, it is those internal debates that lead to the failure of the Church to wield meaningful power in the end. Whether the weakness of the Church as an institution is a disaster, a warning, or a relief the play does not say; the ambiguous ending leaves this as an open question.

CHARACTERS

Each character has a particular motivation, catalyzed by the Crown of Thorns relic. This centralization around a sacred ritual object is common practice in many of Williams's works: the Grail, a magical stone, the Platonic archetypes, a verse play, or a work of art serve as catalysts of spiritual revelation and change. Like the way the crime often serves to expose characters' true natures in a murder mystery, so these material things draw the characters towards themselves, then reveal each person's real spiritual nature by how each reacts to its offered power. Good characters are calm about their relationship to the object: willing to take care of it, use it, let it go, or even destroy it as necessary. Evil characters strive to bend the object to their will: attempting to force it to serve them. In the Arthurian poetry, the Holy Grail serves as this kind of revelatory catalyst, and characters (most notably Galahad) also serve as the centers of revelatory power. Finally, the Empire serves as an image of the Kingdom of God on earth, and the ways in which individual people or countries relate to the Empire shows their true selves and determines their eternal course.

With each new choice of spiritual nucleus in these later works, Williams seems to be reaching further and further behind the veil of material reality, searching for the ultimate Power that created and guides it. Each symbol correspond to some sacred core of existence beyond itself, some mystery even more closely associated with transcendence. Behind the Grail in *War in Heaven* is its keeper, Prester John, who is somehow identified with the Grail, with all true believers, and with Christ Himself. Behind Solomon's magical chunk of original matter in *Many Dimensions* is his signet ring, which contains or is the divine light that made the universe. Behind the tarot cards and the dancing images in *The Greater Trumps* is the Fool, who moves and does not move, and who is the meaning of all things. Behind the angelic orders of Platonic archetypes in *The Place of the Lion* is the Unity, the Three-In-One.

Here in this early work, in 1912, the Crown of Thorns serves a similar purpose, though not as well developed as the ritual objects of the later poetry and fiction. The Crown of Thorns sits, motionless, inside a quiet Chapel by the sea. The surf rumbles gently outside. The Crown of Thorns does not move, but it moves everyone around it. Each character is drawn towards it or fights away from it as his or her spiritual nature yearns towards full expression and fulfillment.

Joachim

Joachim is the Priest of the Chapel of the Holy Thorn. He sits at the center, where the Thorn resides. He is its Keeper and has taken some of its still, submissive, resigned nature into himself. He desires unity and peace among the various factions of the Church, and his knowledge of God is through love, passion, and rapture. He claims: "No man may fear God save as lovers fear" (I.254), and teaches the villagers that one way to know God is through love, romance, desire, and sex—or at least the villagers think that Joachim has been "Teaching that God was in our midst and all / Desire was from [God] and toward him at last" (II:245-46). In Joachim's teachings, then, are the seeds of a strong *Via Affirmativa*. Williams developed his distinctive Romantic Theology after reading the works of A. E. Waite and argued that natural desire, especially romantic or sexual desire, can be interpreted or channeled into true religious devotion. He is a mystic who sees a vision within the Communion cup (II.517-527) and has:

> beheld the holy Bride, the Church,
> Caught to her mystic marriage through the world,
> Wed to her Lover in all mortal things,—
> . . .
> This is the spiritual verity,
> This is the Church, this is salvation, this!
> And will ye make it sure to men by law? (I:927-29, 943-44)

His condemnation of law is the other key to Joachim's character: he desires to teach true freedom, not a dead religion of formalism, rules, and "a lawyer's code" (I.854). Questioning Constantine's devotion, Joachim asks: "Into what law wert thou baptized, O king? / Or rather to what freedom?" (I.542-43) and goes on to press the point: "Are not these poor folk whom God died for, freed / From any law except Christ's pulse in theirs" (I.545-46)? Joachim's interactions with the Thorn reveal his visceral passion for God, his fierce love of freedom, and the complete submission of his will to unfolding events.

Innocent

Innocent is Abbot of the Monastery of St. Cyprian. He wields the power of the Church with abrasive confidence, even brandishing it in the face of king and lesser priest alike. He tells a rich landowner that a poor man, seeking sanctuary in the Chapel, "is surely housed / From temporal hands and secular arrest" (I:364-65), then goes further, overbearing the landowner with proud words:

> Lord, learn thou hast no spearman, gateman, page,
> . . . What say we? . . wife, child, if our lips forbid
> In name of the Church their service. He thy man?
> If thou set foot or speak word more than we
> Allow thee, at due time, damned art thou—damned! (I:376-380).

Here Innocent claims mastery over men's material possessions and eternal souls. Not content to control his merely local villagers, parish priest, and landed gentry, he confronts the king Constantine, daring that monarch to attempt a power struggle with the Church:

> Who is it shall deny our passage? King,
> We are not to be cajoled thus and chid!
> Thou art the Church's servant or her foe:
> Choose. (I:485-88).

Pressured into choosing between the Church and Satan, the king bows to Innocent's force of will and gives in to all of the Abbot's demands. It is with some reason, then, that Innocent can say: "The Church controls at will the secular arm, / Which hath, except thereby, no power to move" (I:514-15).

In addition to being an abbot, Innocent is also a warrior. In the past, before the action of the play, he "drove forth the bards, / Fought, and won battle over rebels and foes, / And now builds convents" (I:179-81). He is a political as well as religious force, and has local, regional, and wide-spread influence.

In direct opposition to Joachim, Innocent is the voice of Law: "custom, law, and use" (I:437). He says of the villagers: "let them pay / Their due of righteous living first to God" (I:553-54). This conflict between Law (Innocent) and Freedom (Joachim) has echoes—admittedly anachronistic echoes in the wrong direction—of Protestant/Catholic debates throughout Church history that are not lost on readers at our chronological remove.

Innocent sees himself as God's vice-regent on earth, dealing out judgment in God's place: "Questionless must the Justicer uphold / All law" (I:422-23) he asserts, and: "I have power to slay, and to release have power" (I:710). While these claims are supported by the evidence—King Constantine gives in to him, after all—Innocent is also a master of words, twisting others to his will by playing with them rhetorically. He is a hard character to grasp, as he slips from one position to another, manipulating the people around him to suit his desires.

For instance, as noted above, Innocent drove out the pagan bards. Yet when he meets Amael, leader of a pagan (quasi-druidic) religion, he greets him thus: "A priest in mine own office, even as thou" (I:679). How surprising, that the Catholic priest with a firm belief in law, even legalism, would greet a pagan poet as a religious equal. Perhaps it is this very ability to suit his words to the situation, to use threats or suavity as the situation demands, that endears him to some readers.

Amael

Amael is a singer and priest of the cult of Druhild: "Last singer and high-priest of this land's gods" (I:113). His religion shares some similarities with Druidism. For instance, his ancient hero is called "Druhild of the Trees" (I:40, 149), he reveres local places (such as the site of the Chapel, since Druhild is buried beneath it), and his faith is pantheistic. His gods are called "the Rider by Night, / The Singer of Strife, the Flame about the Wild!" (I:630-31). He is a harp-player, a wanderer, a poet, and a priest. He is, in short, the prototype of Taliessin in the later Arthurian poetry. Williams gave some of the most beautiful poetry to this singer. Yet Amael is darkly manipulative: threatening, shocking, or sweet-talking others in order to outmatch them all.

Amael's goals are diverse and complex. He wants to gain control of the place where the Chapel is. He wants to make certain that his followers are allowed to worship in that vicinity and to tell tales of Druhild. He wants to ensure that the old gods are not forgotten. He wants the villagers to fight to prevent the Chapel from being walled in, which would keep them from venerating the spot.

At the same time, however, his idea of faith is more subtle than Innocent's. The Abbot believes in external ritual, law, and custom: Amael believes in a faith of the heart, with or without external signs. In fact, he has no problem with hypocrisy, for he says: "Let the people, the poor folk, / Bow down their heads indeed, before the Cross, / But in their hearts remember as they will" (I:150-52). He is content to let the Church have the people's outward conformity as long as his old gods claim their hearts—and their private pleasures. For he believes in desire; he tells Joachim: "I also teach desire, my brother…. / Women for love, vengeance for hate: what more?" (I:255-56).

Amael's religion is more complex than a simple folk Pantheism. In one of the most powerful speeches in the play, he describes what lies behind his ancient gods and heroes:

> There is a darkness beyond all the gods,
> Where once in many ages that which Is
> In Its eternal sleep whose dreams we are
> Heaves suddenly and shudders half-awake.
> Then, as an earthquake rends the seas and shores
> Making all strange, so the All-being moves,
> And all the visible and invisible worlds
> In that sole motion ruin and are re-born
> Into fresh lands, new nations, other gods (I:758-66).

In these few lines, Amael brings up many of the most vexing questions in the history of Western Philosophy, such as the problem of perception, ontological doubts, causation, destiny and self-determinism, the nature and duration of matter, and so on. Similarly, he provokes questions and doubts in the minds of other characters, even at the risk of undermining his own position. For example, although one of his goals is to make sure his people retain enough religious freedom to be allowed to tell tales of Druhild without fear of persecution, yet he taunts Innocent with the power of these stories: "Yet wilt thou leave old stories in their mouths? / Are not they also danger, abbot?" (II:267-68). He wants to score a point even more deeply than he wants to achieve liberty for his people. He wants to have the last word—"To sing a last song" (I:232)—and he almost succeeds in this, for he sings the last song of the play. He does not have the last word, though, and the final meaning of the play must be decided by the reader or director in each subsequent reading or performance.

Michael

Amael's last desire is to seduce young Michael away from the Church. Michael is Joachim's acolyte at the Chapel, but he is sick of serving Jesus: he is

> weary of these prayers and hymns
> And mysteries of the holy bread and wine,

And spiritual visions to be seen
In due time, if I fast and watch the Thorn! (I:64-67)

He longs to travel, to see the world, to experience other people and perspectives: "To pluck from danger glory, gold, or song! / To gain some great hope, some desire of the world!" (II:500-01). He finds himself torn between his priestly father, Joachim, and the pagan priest-bard, Amael. Michael sits in the middle of the whirling conflicts, watching everyone's pettiness and hypocrisy, consumed by *wanderlust*. Music calls to his heart, and he is a visionary:

Last night I dreamed that on this cliff I saw
How the lord abbot strove with Joachim,
Till the earth split beneath them, and they twain
Slipped into darkness, and the Chapel fell. (I:46-49)

His dream is at least metaphorically prophetic.

Amael offers Michael a chance to travel the world as harp-bearer if he will sacrifice Christ and renounce his hereditary position as Keeper of the Thorn in exchange for embracing paganism and poetry. While his decision is not given prominence in terms of number of lines spoken or time spent, it does provide a point of sympathy for the audience in the shape of a real human dilemma dramatized with sympathy and psychological reality.

It is interesting to note that the scansion of Act II, line 533, seems to indicate, by its scansion, that "Michael" is pronounced in the Hebrew fashion, with three syllables.

Gregory

Gregory is the leader of the village. He may be the easiest to sympathize with, because all he wants is to be left alone to try to manage everyday life. When Joachim calls his interests "small" in contrast to the condition of his eternal soul, he exclaims:

Small! it is that we know we have,—a hut,
Talk with our kinsmen, wife or chamber-maid
To keep the hut, a sleeping-place, and food.
Small! it is that we have. (II:393-96)

He and his people struggle against "hunger, plague, / War, tax of labour" (I:182-83)—essentially, death and taxes. Measured against this "stream of life,"

The thought of God is like a rooted weed
Which drags a little at the surface-flow
But dams not any current. (II:443-46)

He is loyal to Druhild, but really does not care what the bigger men fight over and decide, as long as:

...this place should still
Be open to us village men, a priest

> Being from the convent sent here to sing mass
> And be a watchman by it; that no law
> Should exile tales of Druhild with the bards (II:181-85).

He is a functional pluralist, thinking that beliefs have little practical effect in any case:

> But wheresoever we bow down or no,
> Yea, though we bow down or we bow not down,
> Still are we hungered when the harvest fails,
> Thirsty with labour, sun-burnt, chill with rain. (I:207-10)

Although he had originally promised to fight on behalf of Joachim to protect the Chapel of the Thorn from the Abbot's grasping machinations, he decides that "meat and drink are older than belief / And sleep than faith more needful" (II:464-65). And he gets what he wants in the end. The kings and priests leave him alone. He can go on living.

Constantine

The last significant character is a king named Constantine. His appearance in the narrative could suggest a more specific chronological identification than the vague reference above to "somewhere between the third and fifth centuries A.D." Is this character meant to be the Emperor Constantine the Great (r. 306-337)? He did visit Britain in 305 A.D. and was crowned in York after his father's death (Geoffrey 132).[12]

Yet identifying the Constantine of *Chapel* with the historical Constantine I ("the Great") is problematic, for one strong reason: How can this petty, disrespected, impotent character be the glorious Emperor of Williams's later Byzantium? In *The Chapel of the Thorn*, Constantine is a minor character without pomp, circumstance, or respect. His entrance onto the stage goes unnoticed by the others. The Abbot Innocent does not shrink from confronting him, even telling him what to do and making demands of him. Innocent threatens resignation, and Constantine gives in; he bows to Innocent's local power. Throughout the play, he is very easily persuaded and very little honored.

In the later Arthurian poetry, on the other hand, the Emperor represents the operative work of God's kingdom on earth and serves the symbolic function of God Himself; "The throne-room of the Emperor of Byzantium… typifies the presence of God" (Lewis, "Williams and the Arthuriad" 291). It is hard to imagine the Constantine of *Chapel* typifying anything awe-inspiring or even admirable.

Here is another suggestion. Is this character meant to be the local sixth-century King Constantine III of Britain, the one castigated by Gildas and listed by Geoffrey of Monmouth as successor to King Arthur? Is he "This horrid abomination, Constantine, the tyrannical whelp of the unclean lioness of Damonia" (Gildas 40)? His character seems to fit *Chapel*'s Constantine. It would also be lovely to have the Constantine of *Chapel* as the successor to King Arthur: that would provide a potential connection between this early play and the later Arthurian poetry. According to Geoffrey, this local king Constantine III was Arthur's cousin who received the crown from his uncle in 542 A.D. (Geoffrey 261). He is a bad king, "struck down by the vengeance of God" after murdering two young men inside a church (Geoffrey 262). He seems an ideal choice for the weak, easily manipulated king of *Chapel* who is used merely as a placeholder for abstract secular power moved about like a pawn by the far more powerful Church.

However, there is one serious problem with this identification. *The Chapel of the Thorn* is set before the fall of Rome, so the time period is wrong for Constantine III of Britain. "When Rome Falls" is a folk saying among the villagers in the play (II.88), approximately equivalent to "When pigs fly" or "When hell freezes over"; that Fall is still so far in the future that it cannot be imagined by these characters. The white glory of Rome and Rome's spiritual primacy are a distant but powerful force just outside the margins of the text. Therefore, the tale must not be set in the middle of the sixth century, nearly a hundred years after Rome's gradual decline.

There is a third historical candidate in Geoffrey's "History": Constantine II of Britain, father of Uther Pendragon and grandfather of King Arthur. According to Geoffrey, he was sent to protect Britain after the withdrawal of Roman forces, and was greeted by the Archbishop with great enthusiasm: "Christ is victorious! …Christ is King! Christ rules of us! If only Christ is on our side, then you are the King of a deserted Britain! You are our defense, our hope, our joy!" (Geoffrey 150).This account compares favorably with Amael's speech about Constantine in the play:

> …your king
> Came with the Cross-banner, and all his host,—
> And on a day their last bedizened chief
> Stood up beyond his city, in the hills,
> When all his house and bards were slain, and he
> Even while his sword swung over Constantine. (I:115-20)

Then he had three sons: Constans, Aurelius Ambrosius, and Utherpendragon (Geoffrey 151). This Constantine conquered his enemies, gathered together the scattered Britons, and reigned for ten years before being assassinated by "a certain Pict" (Geoffrey 151).

The play is set seven years into Constantine's reign; Amael says: "And the third year the king went forth to war, / And warred three years more; and for twelve months since / Hath built a convent for his thanks to God" (I:167-69). Dodds observes: "all the coming troubles up to and through the reign of Uther and until the rise of Arthur might be conceived of as possibly looming in the not-too-distant future after the end of the action of *The Chapel*. All of which, if true, would make The Chapel an allusive and very 'understated' sort of Arthurian prologue" (Dodds "Another Constantine!").

This is delightful. Knowing Williams's later poetry, this reader at least would *like* the Constantine of *Chapel* to be either Arthur's grandfather or Arthur's heir. But if wishes were horses…. And neither a supposition nor a preference good scholarship makes. Of course, Williams did not know in 1912 what he would go on to write (even though he was already obsessed with the Arthurian legends), so it is not very helpful to look back on this play through the lens of poems written twenty-six years later.

What, then, are we to make of all this? Which Constantine is intended in the play? Or why doesn't Williams make the identification clearer? There are at least two possible answers to this perplexing question of the identification of Constantine in *Chapel*.

First, Williams nurtured a remarkable attitude towards the flexibility of time, believing in the simultaneity of all times. He did not envision time as unrolling in historical order or as proceeding along a line; instead, he saw times as dynamically interacting, intersecting, and overlapping according to a spiritual logic beyond the human perception of linearity. In the later Arthurian poetry, his Empire is an imaginary combination of the Roman and Byzantine empires, without the Church's East-West split, into which he conflates events from before 410 A.D. until 1453. I believe that Williams either suggests that Arthur's reign covered that entire period, or he compresses a historical millennium down into King Arthur's lifetime. This is something more than creative anachronism; Williams does not merely put (for instance) stirrups and cavalry back into the sixth century or the Battle of Mount Badon forward into the fifteenth; rather, events from widely separated historical periods happen simultaneously in the spiritual economy of Logres. Whatever events are necessary to carry the symbolism and significance of Arthur's kingdom occur within it in Williams's retelling, regardless of when they "actually" occurred on the dusty line of historical time (Higgins "Double Affirmation" 61).

Therefore, this Constantine in *Chapel* could be the Briton Constantine III from 542, imported backwards into Roman Britannia in order to reveal the susceptibility of secular power to corruption and to show how quickly Arthur's "once and shining moment" passed into disrepute, or he could be a conflation of elements from two or three of these historical personages, chosen for the characterological and theological purposes Williams desired.

The second possibility is that this character is none of the historical Constantines, but merely another person of the same name. The name evokes "constant, steadfast," and impresses a reader with a sense of power and authority so that his failures as a ruler are all the more ironic and poignant.

That, then, is a survey of the major characters in *The Chapel of the Thorn* and their motivations. There are a few other minor characters, including Theodoric: an angry, violent, self-absorbed landowner. He wants what he calls "justice": vengeance on a man who killed his horse. But even he has larger schemes, which are only revealed in his last three lines.

Analysis

There is a startlingly strong sympathy for the non-Christian perspective throughout this drama. The play ends with a stirring dual anthem. The priests chant Christian texts in Latin while Amael and the villagers sing a rousing ballad and folksong about Druhild.

I have left out one minor but essential character: the one who gets the last words. An unnamed woman gets the last word, praising the Virgin Mary for healing her son. The overwhelming sense of the ending is indeterminate. Christian and Pagan sing to their gods. The Christian song is high poetical Latin; Amael's song is a lively rhythmical ballad. Who wins?

Nobody wins. Or everybody wins.

After a reading or performance of the play, an audience would be left ponder those last words: what they are, who said them, and the circumstances surrounding their utterance. Choices made by a theater or film director would have far-reaching interpretive consequences. At what point the music stopped, where the characters were standing, their tones of voice, their posture and gestures—all of these theatrical decisions would express an interpretation of the play, especially an opinion about who wins the conflict in the end.

If the monks continue their chant until the curtain falls, then the Abbot Innocent wins with his formalist Christianity. If the villagers keep singing their song of Druhild, then paganism and the common people win. If Amael's heroic ballad continues beyond the final lines, then he wins. If the music cuts off before the last lines so that the woman's prayer to Mary is spoken into the silence, then a Christianity of freedom and of the common people wins.

Who speaks for Charles Williams? Is any one character the voice of the author? The play creates such a delicate balance among opposing forces that it seems he agrees with everyone, or no one. Gregory achieves his goal: non-interference for his villagers. Amael achieves his: access to the Chapel ground and to the people's ears and hearts. Innocent achieves his: control of the Thorn. What about Joachim? He loses—unless his real point was not about the Thorn, but about grace and about not giving the others anything they want for their own reasons. If that is the case, perhaps his apparent failure is success. Is Williams, then, advocating unfettered freedom? Or paganism? Or legalism? Or withdrawal from the world?

The text does not allow any of these interpretations—or rather, it allows all of them, simultaneously, in a kind of indeterminate pluralism. This drama is a venue for playing with all of the philosophies, trying each one on, speaking in the voice of each character, and finding out some of the implications—in thought and in action—of each idea. Asking whether Williams himself was actively trying on each of these belief systems in writing *The Chapel of the Thorn* is a fairly fruitless question; however, for all its limitations, considering biographical context might lead a reader to wonder whether the young Williams was raising spiritual questions, facing doubts, pondering the truth of Christianity, and considering agnosticism, syncretism, or relativism.

In his one published work from this same time, *The Silver Stair,* the narrative persona is struggling to decide whether to affirm or deny romantic, sexual love. Williams presented the book to his girlfriend, Florence Conway, in January between 1909 and 1911 (most likely 1910; cf. Hadfield *Exploration* 16). She read the poems and, perspicacious girl, wondered if they meant he was going to join a monastery. Instead, they became engaged and remained engaged for nine years while Charles wrestled with the competing claims of the Way of Affirmation and the Way of Negation. He decided in favor of Affirmation. In 1917, Williams married Florence. He nicknamed her "Michal." They had one son, whom they named Michael.

Michael is the name of the young apostate in this play, written ten years before Michael Williams was born. Of course, Williams and his wife did not name their son after the character in this play: they named him after the Archangel. Williams wrote to Pellow: "I have been instructing Michael in his patron, but when he says 'What's he like?' I hesitate to make him human in shape: so I say – 'He is light and fire'" (qtd. in Dodds "Some notes on names").

Yet Charles Williams was still circulating this play two years after his son's birth, in 1924, when he sent it to Pellow (and perhaps tried to get it published). The name was, then, still in his mind. Perhaps he sympathized with this character's dilemma.

Williams was a committed Anglican Christian all his life, in spite of (or along with, or possibly even because of) his ten years in the Fellowship of the Rosy Cross. The creeds and sacraments were essential to his mental processes, and he seems never to have considered any change, either to another denomination or to anything outside of Christianity. He did not get involved in internal church debates. He wrote the East/West Schism of 1054 out of his re-imagined Arthurian history. Although he was deeply involved in an occult secret society, he appears to have taken the occult into his faith-system, rather than vice-versa.

I have found no external evidence that Williams ever went through an experience of conversion to Christianity, as Lewis did, or serious commitment, as Tolkien did. It appears that he grew up into his faith in much the same way he grew up into language, literature, Englishness, or anything else he took for granted as an essential feature of his identity. Yet *The Chapel of the Thorn* suggests that he may have gone through a serious period of doubt that resolved itself slowly.

Doubt is an essential part of Williams's system of thought. It was planted in his mind from an early age. On long walks, his father engaged him in profound debates, always encouraging him to consider all sides of an argument, and even to switch sides regularly to see what it felt like on a different side. Carpenter records that Charles' father:

> was not only widely-read but totally undogmatic, teaching his son that there were many sides to every argument, and that it was necessary to understand the elements of reason in the other point of view as well as your own. Though a devout churchman, he encouraged Charles to appreciate the forces of atheist rationalism…. his father had taught him to absorb doubt and disbelief into his beliefs. (Carpenter 77)

This habit of striving to understand all sides of an argument, including the outside, appears to have stayed with him all his life. Williams expresses thanks for this ability in an early poem (1920):

> I will of doubt make such an art
> That no dismay shall move
> Sufficient bitterness of heart
> For unbelief in love. ("First Love" ll. 13-16, *Divorce* 49)

Windows of Night (1925) contains a remarkable poem entitled "To the Protector, or Angel, of Intellectual Doubt," which proposes that Faith and Doubt are twin sisters who are necessary to one another's existence (pp. 105-113). The evidence of his books and letters suggests that "he maintained a strong skepticism… by which he meant not a denial of dogma, but a delicately balanced ambiguity between what one can know and what one believes" (Edwards 45; cf. Hadfield *Exploration* 20). Cavaliero calls this quality an "absolute relativism" (ix) or deep humility about how much human intellect can know for sure.

The ideas about doubt and faith in *Chapel of the Thorn*, then, are at the heart of Williams's developing thought about what belief was, what it excluded, and what it included. In fact, as I hope to show below, this little play contains many of his most important ideas, more or less developed.

Dramatic Potential

The Chapel of the Thorn, then, is a worthy piece of writing to show Williams's development as a poet and playwright, to reveal his early state of mind, and to raise interesting questions about the nature of belief and of sacred objects. It is also an interesting study of several dynamic characters involved in a focused conflict.

But is it any good? Is the poetry good? Is it a good drama? Is it playable on the modern stage?

I am happy to report that the answer to all of these questions is Yes. On March 17th, 2014 (St. Patrick's Day), eight members of my local artists'-and-writers' fellowship gathered with me in a church basement to read the entire play out loud. Act I took nearly fifty-six minutes to read; Act II took just over forty-one minutes. Each participant was assigned one of the eight major characters and one or more of the minor roles. We made an audio recording of the reading, and we had a lively, intelligent discussion of the play between the two acts and at the end.

The unanimous response to this event was that *The Chapel of the Thorn* contains beautiful poetry, engaging characters, emotional depth, real conflict, compelling drama, and an exciting narrative arc—and that it could and should be produced. It also requires only a small cast, minimal sets, and limited technical magic, which make it a practical choice. The director of a local youth theater was present, along with two of her assistant directors and several actors. The theater director stated unequivocally that she could see this play being performed and may be interested in mounting a production herself in future. All the others with theatrical experience concurred. No one was bored; everyone was engaged by the action. Each person had a different character with whom he or she sympathized, and we had a lively debate about the ending of the play. Many of the insights in this essay were clarified, deepened, or born in that conversation. Most importantly, hearing the poetry read aloud by a variety of voices was a very powerful experience. Given the right director and cast, *The Chapel of the Thorn* could be quite a successful play.

That is not to say it is without problems. It is infected with the sexism and racism common in the works of early 20th-century bourgeois Englishmen—along with odd references by Amael and the villagers to the "white Christ." These appear to be derogatory statements about His apparent weakness, as compared to the warrior-heroes they venerate, rather than ethnic references. In II:138, Amael calls the virgin Mary "the pale goddess." This seems to indicate that he is using "the white Christ" as an insult without racial valance, suggesting that Christ is pale with fear.

There is only one female character, and she is given no name and only ten lines. True, she speaks the final (and thus, arguably, most important) line of the play, but she functions as a place-holder for simple faith, rather than as a person in her own right.[13] The eight major characters are all male. Of course, given the historical setting of this play and its concerns with sacred and secular power, it is inevitable that all the kings and priests (at least on the Christian side) must be men. A pagan priestess would have been a fascinating choice, but the added gender dynamics would distract from the tensions that Williams designed the play to explore. Perhaps some daring director will cast a woman as Amael at some point in the future—but I do not recommend that for a first performance, as the play needs to be seen as Williams wrote it.

Besides that one "woman," the only other women referred to are all off stage, never spoken of by name, and treated as possessions for the men to buy, sell, trade, and abuse as they please. The villagers have a practice of "sale betwixt ourselves of chamber-maids" (I:21). Two men have a conversation about a "lusty" young maid that one wants to sell, and the other says he will consider buying her if a free meal is thrown into the bargain (I:28-32). These village men are entirely pragmatic about the women they have objectified: each needs to make sure he has a "wife or chamber-maid / To keep the hut" (II:394-95). To be fair, this practice of buying and selling female slaves as concubines is frowned upon by Innocent, and so cannot be directly attributed to Williams without further evidence. Joachim's position is not clear; one villager is not sure, but thinks he heard Joachim "Teaching that God was in our midst and all / Desire was from him and toward him at last" (II:245-46), and interpreted this to mean that all sexual desire and behavior were blessed by the church.

Obviously, these are the characters speaking, and it would be premature to assign such comments to Williams himself. There is a kind of inherent patriarchalism in the ways in which he describes Romantic Theology in other works, suggesting that the woman is always the means, and the man's salvation the end, but a much more detailed study of his writings than I will indulge in here would be necessary to clear or accuse him of the charge of essential sexism.[14]

The issue of racism in *Chapel of the Thorn* is similar. There are horrific statements, such Michael's desire to travel and see "Kings who have black men for their cup-bearers, / And yellow-featured slant-eyed slaves for guard" (I:86-87). Again, however, this is Michael speaking, not Williams. His later works are remarkably inclusive, especially *Many Dimensions*, in which the salvific religion is (at least superficially) Islam, and the Arthurian poetry, in which a "Moslem" knight comes to understand truth via such varied teachers as "Talaat ibn Kula of Ispahan," Euclid, Archimedes, Coelius Vibenna, romantic love, and Jewish Cabbalism. Again, there are opportunities for a larger study of Williams's depiction of Islam and of ethnic minorities.[15]

There are a few other technical difficulties that would also make a production of this play challenging. I do not think Williams ever heard it read aloud. The sentences are too long. The lengthy speeches are difficult to perform and to understand. There are too many characters standing around without saying anything while others deliver enormous, uninterrupted monologues. There is the possibility (which Lindop mentions in the preface to this volume, p. 1) that *Chapel* was intended as a closet drama: for reading, not for performance. Perhaps someone should make an adaptation in which a few of the speeches are shortened, or other lines are given to the silent characters as punctuation for the monologues. Perhaps it would succeed even better as a film, because camera work could heighten the interest of a long speech and serve as an interpretive mechanism.

Yet the strengths of this short work far outweigh its weaknesses. The poetry is beautiful. The drama is real. It is very plot- and character-driven, and takes the viewer on a roller coaster of character arcs. The audience is caught up in the weaving in and out of words. In the first act, the characters are mostly static, but their motivations are slowly revealed. There is plenty of dialog, back and forth like a tennis match, and there are also many long monologues in which good actors could shine. In the second act, elements become more chaotic, building to a tempest of speech and sound at the end—before all becomes clear and silent at the last moment. The sound of the sea is always murmuring in the background.

One impressive production possibility would be to take a cue from some of Williams's later dramas and stage *Chapel* as an elaborate Masque. This play is built against a backdrop of high ceremonial and striking ritual, so those elements should be brought into the sets and staging. There could be much music throughout, from Latin hymns and chants to wild pagan folksongs and atmospheric music highlighting characters' states of mind and the interactions of nature. Amael, as singer of Druhild, could sing many of his lines, and the priests could employ chant or recitative for their most powerful moments. Characters should enter the stage in the midst of high processionals, and their blocking should be beautifully choreographed, almost dance-like in their movements and interactions. Fully executed dances—of villagers, probably—could be used as interludes. The visuals should be striking and memorable, using bold colors for the priests' vestments and accessories.

All of these multi-media elements would build up to an actual conflict between the groups, a squaring-off of forces, as a clarification, before the final narrowing of the chaos into silence. This approach would need to be carefully balanced with a director's sensitive ear to the flights of poetic beauty: no clutter (visual, auditory, or kinesthetic) should interfere with the pure sublimity of some of the speeches. At those moments, all else should fall silent and still, in order to let those lines of ecstatic iambic pentameter fill the air. And still the sound of the sea would always murmur in the background.

COMPARISON TO OTHER EARLY WORKS

The Silver Stair (1912)

1912, the year *Chapel* was completed, is the same year that Williams first had a book published.[16] It is *The Silver Stair*, a cycle of eighty-four sonnets, published in London by Herbert & Daniel with the support of Alice and Wilfrid Meynell.

The Silver Stair is a well-structured volume of verse whose strengths of organization and narrative power have been overlooked because of the derivative and sometimes mannered structure of these sonnets. It is true that Williams does use fairly rigid rhyme schemes, conventional metrical patterns, and archaic diction in this volume. He would continue to do so all the way until *Taliessin through Logres* (1938), which bears the marks of his editing of Hopkins (Ridler lxi, Cavaliero 98, Dunning 112, Higgins and Talbot 64, Moorman 108). Yet he handles these elements of form and style deftly. His profundity of thought and skillful management of poetic technique in even his earliest works should be noted.

The lines of iambic pentameter in *Chapel of the Thorn* are less regular than those in *The Silver Stair*. Perhaps this is intended to make them more conversational, more dramatic. Yet while the regularity of *The Silver Stair* feels juvenile, derivative, and immature, the irregularities of *The Chapel of the Thorn* sound unprofessional and unpolished.[17] In both, the overall impression is that Williams had not yet found his poetic voice. But the juvenile nature of both of these works has been overstated. While they are not the masterpieces of the 1930s and 40s, they are powerful, original works of verse.

The Silver Stair follows the theological and literary pattern that Williams would later postulate in *Outlines of Romantic Theology*, matching up the stages of romantic love with the earthly life of Christ. There is none of that in *Chapel*, although the centrality of the relic suggests the importance of objects in focusing religions devotion, and points to an Affirmative use of image. Yet Joachim's final surrender could be read as an act of negation corresponding to the startlingly clear *Via Negativa* explored in *The Silver Stair*. The young writer appears to have been torn between the two Ways, struggling to decide which to follow.

The Silver Stair also carries strong hints of the way Williams would live his life according to a myth, as the narrator assigns roles to himself and everyone he encounters, giving them parts to play in his grand saga of chivalry. This attitude partly explains Williams's approach to characterization: "his theological purpose led him to depict characters, in Platonic terms, as copies of absolute spiritual realities" rather than as fully-developed three-dimensional people (Higgins "Christian Mystery" 80). The subordination of individuals to their roles is somewhat apparent in *Chapel*—but, as discussed above, the characters are quite lively and dynamic.

As there is in *Chapel,* there is also an undertone of doubt, questioning, and lack of faith in *The Silver Stair*. There is some sense of world-weariness, as the narrator occasionally expresses a worn-out, indifferent attitude towards life—at least before falling in love: "Day and Night / Offend us with an equal weariness" ("The predestined lover" ll. 1-2, *Silver Stair* 3). This seems similar to Gregory's attitude towards the beginning of *Chapel*:

> But wheresoever we bow down or no,
> Yea, though we bow down or we bow not down,
> Still are we hungered when the harvest fails,
> Thirsty with labour, sun-burnt, chill with rain.
> Gods change, and we: yet little is to change. (I:207-11)

Yet these comparisons are not meant to suggest that the two books are at all similar, nor that they are exploring the same range of ideas.

For example, in these two early books, Williams demonstrates opposite uses of the "myth" found in the New Testament Gospels. In *The Silver Stair*, he uses the Gospel story as an allegory for his own love-narrative. He maps each stage of the personal, human love-story onto an episode of the earthly life, death, and resurrection of Christ.

In *Chapel*, on the other hand, he uses pagan religion as another way of telling the same one true story of cyclical regeneration. In this way, he seems to prefigure the great "True Myth" narratives of his later associates, Lewis, Tolkien, and—to a lesser extent—Barfield, who saw in the patterns of fertility religions and seasonal myths a foreshadowing, a metaphor, or even a prophecy of the historical Passion of Christ.[18]

Note that Williams had developed his version of the "true myth" idea before he met the Inklings. Innocent gives a variation of it in the following lines:

> Thou that hast not begun to learn of Christ,
> Canst thou tell what tales hide within that word?
> Or how or when we priests, his vagrant bards,
> To slaves, to freemen, or to kings should teach
> His name; wherein all thoughts of Druhild move,
> Because it is the folklore of the world? (II:271-76)

The Gospel is the folklore of the world.... This is a more startling way of saying what Paul says in Romans chapter 1 about God being revealed to all the world through His creation. Innocent seems to be arguing that general revelation includes knowledge of Christ, specifically, not merely of God the Father. This is rather shocking. And when Innocent puts forward a universalist doctrine a few lines later, Amael retorts:

> Thou ravest. Shall one alien or one dead
> Be by a faith he hath not known redeemed? (II:315-16)

And Innocent replies:

> No man hath lived who hath not known the Faith. (II:317).

This is an extreme application of the idea of true myth, and one that probably would have horrified Lewis and Tolkien—and probably the Church authorities, too.[19] But *Chapel* does not give a definitive statement that either the Christian Gospel fulfills the hints of pagan myths or that the Christian Gospel is just another such myth. The action leaves both possibilities open.

The Arthurian Commonplace Book (c. 1912-c. 1923?)

1912 is also the year in which Williams began keeping a notebook of thoughts, ideas, and clippings related to the development of his great Grail myth. This compendium of ideas on the King Arthur and Grail stories has come to be called the *Arthurian Commonplace Book*.[20] While the dating of this notebook is inexact, "We can guess when the volume was started because Williams used a 'publisher's dummy' from the Press – one of the full-sized volumes, full of blank pages, which publishers used to try out possible bindings when producing a book" (Lindop, *The Last Magician*). This particular dummy was left over from work on *The Concise Oxford Dictionary*, which was first published in 1911. These notebooks "would have been lying about the offices of the OUP in that year, or just before, and they would have been redundant when the book appeared. Williams must have helped himself to one" (Lindop). In other words, Williams must have started the *Commonplace Book* no earlier than 1910 and no later than 1912. Notes and clippings in the book also indicate that he "he began seriously collecting material for 'His epic, his King Arthur' around 1912. Newspaper clippings pasted in later suggest that he continued to pack material into the thick blank book until at least 1915" (Lindop). David Dodds writes that "one could suggest that *CB* was compiled largely …in the two years between January 1913 and February 1915, and added to over the next year or two" or perhaps largely "between March 1914 and November 1916"; other evidence he mentions suggests Williams may have continued working in it as late as 1923 (Dodds, "Intro").

What is most fascinating for the current study is that Williams mentions or alludes to *The Chapel of the Thorn* four times in the *Commonplace Book*. On page 19, he quotes from it, but with a change: the *Commonplace Book* mentions "the 'lust of cruelty in lovers' hands'"; the actual quote from *Chapel* is: "The lust of cruelty in their masters' hands" (II:284). This occurs in a discussion of the Fisher-King's wound and the subsequent wasting of the land; Williams wonders whether the cruelty of nature is like the cruelty of sexual lust.

On page 109, Williams is wresting with ideas about free will and divine will, and especially with the question of how Christ could have two wills and yet be one person. In this context, he quotes exactly from *Chapel*: "He hath created to free use of will / Have therein separate being" (I:729-30), without the line break or the slash, but in quotation marks and with correct capitalization. This suggests to me that he had the MS of *Chapel* at hand and was copying directly from it.

On page 117 of the *Commonplace Book*, Williams imagines a letter from Pope Leo to King Arthur: a "letter on the nature of Love." In it, these lines appear:

> Sorrow working in them
> as yeast in dough   that all ye may be
> Made into white bread for ~~the mouth of God~~ God's mouth to touch

Dodds has a footnote here relating these lines to the following from Chapel, spoken by Joachim:

> But yet through prayer for channel drop by drop
> The slowly oozing waters of man's will
> May fill the chalice of his being, God
> Holds out beneath, until when it be full
> He lift it to His mouth, against whose lip
> Water to wine and virtue to desire
> Flushes in one rare rapture. (II:423-29)

The similarity, of course, is the idea of God eating and drinking His people as bread and wine—an inversion of the Communion imagery of His people participating in His flesh and blood in the bread and wine.

The final *Chapel* reference comes on page 134 of the *Commonplace Book*, where Williams wrote in quotation marks: "so once through chaos — so on Calvary." These words appear in *Chapel* thus: "So once through Chaos, so on Calvary" (II:387). Here Williams was working out the idea that Christ's birth and His passion "are really one," that "the agony of men — Mary in labour — the bearing of Christ — the birth of the new moment in the world." He speculates, "if Eve had asked the question 'How can these things be?' would there have been a fall?" This juxtaposition of "Eve" from Genesis with Perceval from Chrétien de Troyes's romances explicitly associates the Arthurian legend with theological history. In Chrétien's Arthurian romance *Le Conte du Graal*, Perceval comes to the Grail castle. There, during dinner, he sees a procession in which a shining lance, a serving bowl, and a silver serving platter are carried reverently: "As each course was served, he saw the bowl pass before them completely uncovered, but did not know who was served from it, and he would have liked to know" (380). Nor does he ask "why that drop of blood gushes from the gleaming point of the lancehead" (396). Later, it turns out that because of his failure to ask this question, "many knights will die; and lands will be laid waste" (397). By associating Eve with the question "How can these things be?", Williams conflates Biblical history and Arthurian romance: putting Eve in the Grail Castle and Perceval in the Garden of Eden simultaneously, using each of them as a representative of humankind. Each is responsible to do or not to do one thing: To ask the right question, or not to eat the forbidden fruit. Each fails in the mysterious task, humanity falls into sin, the land is laid waste, and the king lies ill. Each must await a truer Knight, a better King, Who will restore the Waste Land and bring redemption.

What do these four quotations from the *Commonplace Book* about *The Chapel of the Thorn* have in common? Nothing superficial or obvious. I suggest that their correspondences have to do with Williams's attempts to work out the relations among Christian doctrine, myth, and history, and to find images sufficient to bear the meanings he saw in all three.

It is clear, then, that Williams was working on—or working through —three major sets of ideas in the 19-teens: affirmation and negation; the Arthurian and Grail legends; and a complex involving holy relics, the Church's civil power, and syncretism. *The Silver Stair* deploys them lyrically, through the persona of a stylized or symbolic Lover. The *Arthurian Commonplace Book* explores them through notes, jottings, and free associations. And *The Chapel of the Thorn* brings them to life through poetry and drama.

Seeds of Future Themes

As discussed above, *The Chapel of the Thorn* was composed during the phase in which Williams was trying to find his poetic style. However, many of his distinctive ideas are already present in nascent form, even though *Chapel* was composed before his courtship and marriage; before he spent ten years in A. E. Waite's Rosicrucian secret society; before he experienced fatherhood; before he became a notable lecturer; before he edited Hopkins' poems or saw the first English translations of Kierkegaard into print; and before his crucial final six years as a member of The Inklings—all those experiences that honed and clarified his thoughts and (more dramatically) his style. It is quite surprising, then, to find that Williams was already working on the ideas that would later make his mature works utterly distinctive. This raises the essential question of source criticism: where did he get his ideas? If not from the Rosicrucians or from the Inklings, then where did he derive his strange blend of hermetic, Christian, and mythological ideas?

All the evidence suggests that Williams's mental life was conducted as a series of recognitions. Rather than learning new ideas from each author he encountered or acquaintance he made, he appears to have conceived at least the germ of each concept, then recognized it in someone else's writings or conversation and gone on to mature it in concert with continued contact with that other thinker. Williams himself claims this in relation to his distinctive, Dantean "Romantic Theology," writing that his early books of poetry are "proof that I developed my own view of romantic love by myself, and not through reading Dante" (letter to Phyllis Potter, February 14th, 1945, qtd. in Hadfield, *Exploration* 34). My suspicion is that he ultimately derived his ideas from an idiomatic reading of Scripture and in conversation with his father, interpreting standard doctrine in nonstandard ways without even realizing that his versions were oddly orthodox at best. Each of his signature ideas seems to have proceeded according to this chronology: he derived the seed of a strange idea from youthful reading and conversation, developed it to a previously unexplored extreme in the oddity of his own mind, expressed it in his writings, and only then encountered other—usually tamer—orthodox versions of these same ideas in the writings of new authors or in the company of new friends. What follows is an examination of each of his peculiar concepts as it appears in *Chapel* and in comparison with later works.

Coinherence, Substitution, and Exchange

Coinherence is at the heart of Williams's system of thought. This is the basic Christian belief that the persons of the Trinity coexist with and in each other, followed by the much more unusual belief that people can carry one another's emotional or spiritual burdens as surely and simply as carrying a box or bag: "Compacts can be made for the taking over of the suffering of troubles, and worries, and distresses, as simply and effectually as an assent is given to the carrying of a parcel" ("The Way of Exchange" 151-2). If you have cancer, for instance, and are terrified of pain and death, Williams believed that you could go to a friend and make a "contract" with that friend so that he or she would "carry" that fear instead of you. You would then find that you were unable to be afraid, even if you tried, no matter how ravaging the disease and how close death came. He even implies that the friend could exchange his life for yours: take on the cancer and die in your place.

This concept finds its origins in two ideas. On the one hand, Williams reached back to theological teachings about the *perichoresis*, in which the Persons of the Trinity co-exist in a kind of eternal dance of love, and to the doctrine of the "hypostatic union" of the persons of Christ (Cavaliero viii, Newman 6). On the other hand, there is the historical-biographical reality that Williams was disqualified from military service in World War I, which meant his friends went to France and died that he might live.[21] "It seemed to Williams," writes Thomas Howard, "that here was a principle. Everyone, all the time, owes his life to others…. There is no such thing as life that does not owe itself to the life and labor of someone else" (Howard 25, 26). So far, this seems an ordinary enough Christian doctrine or even nice human sentiment. Yet Howard, for all his clarity of thought and expression, commits the fault of many Williams scholars: he sanitizes and tames what is utterly wild in Williams's original text.

Part of the wildness was expressed in the founding of an order for the practice of substitution and exchange, which Williams did at the insistence of his disciples in 1939 (Hadfield 173-4; Newman 8). He named this group the Companions of the Coinherence. He composed a document called the "Promulgation of the Company," which lays out the principles of the Order. Here, he wrote that the order recommends "the study…on the active side, of methods of exchange, in the State, in all forms of love, and in all natural things, such as childbirth" (Lang-Sims 30; Hadfield 173-4). In this Promulgation, he enjoins members to carry one another's burdens. As leader of the Order—whom some members called "Master"—he literally ordered them about, telling them who would carry whose burdens.

There is a little bit of evidence suggesting that he occasionally carried some burdens for others himself. Thelma Shuttleworth recounts one such occasion when she was nervous and frightened. She called Williams on the phone, and "We had a conversation like that of Peter Stanhope and Pauline in *Descent into Hell*. Come to think of it, our conversations must usually have sounded like those in his novels." She explained her fears to him, and he said "that I was not to worry, he would see to that. I must simply attend to my affairs, setting all in order and then leaving it to Love. […]All will be most well …. And it was, instantly!" (Shuttleworth 6). On another occasion, Lois Lang-Sims "firmly requested him to 'carry' for me my trepidation at the prospect of teaching the Sunday school" (Lang-Sims 58). Williams replied that he would lay himself open to "being scared" in her place, "And you will leave it to me" (59)[22]

In 1941, Williams wrote a more thorough explanation of this Way of life and thought: "The Way of Exchange," which was first published as a pamphlet in the *New Foundations* series in 1941 (and is now found most readily in *The Image of the City*, 147-154). These concepts of Coinherence, Substitution, and Exchange are most clearly expressed in his last and greatest works, especially the novel *Descent Into Hell* (1937) and the Arthurian poetry (*Taliessin through Logres*, 1938, and *The Region of the Summer Stars*, 1944). However, there is an early hint of co-inherence and exchange in *The Chapel of the Thorn*.[23] One character says that the priest, Joachim, grows old:

> with a greater weight
> Than all his days upon him, for he bears
> The times of twain his brethren, they who died
> In the great plague, last followers of his creed. (I:155-58)

Two of Joachim's brother priests died of the plague, but Joachim went on living. It appears that he feels as if their deaths were given in exchange for his life, and he bears the burden of this substitution. Whether this burden is guilt or a sense of responsibility, or both, is not specified. Either way, Joachim is the *recipient* of a gift of exchange, rather than the giver, and he finds the gift burdensome. Notice that this is a more negative view of exchange than we find in Williams's later works. Interesting, too, that he wrote this before two of his best friends, Harold Eyers and Ernest Nottingham, were killed in action in World War One (Hadfield 23, 25). This is but one example of the many ways in which, during the 19-teens and -twenties, Williams was just beginning to work out what would become his distinctive system of thought.

THE REVELATORY SACRAL OBJECT

Williams's most popular works are his seven novels: *War in Heaven* (1930), *Many Dimensions* (1931), *The Place of the Lion* (1931), *The Greater Trumps* (1932), *Shadows of Ecstasy* (published in 1933 but written first), *Descent into Hell* (1937), and *All Hallow's Eve* (1945). In each novel, sacramental objects or occult adepts unleash spiritual forces that threaten vast temporal or spiritual destruction. This idea of a central point to which all people and actions are drawn is another important theme throughout his works. It is expressed most clearly in the novels and the Arthurian poetry, but also discussed elsewhere and hinted at in *Chapel of the Thorn*.

In *Many Dimensions*, the sacred object is a magical stone from the crown of Solomon. It has powers of time travel, spatial transportation, and healing. By the ways in which they desire to use this stone, characters reveals themselves as protagonists or antagonists. In *The Greater Trumps*, the sacral objects are a pack of Tarot cards and a corresponding set of golden images. Their union is supposed to grant ultimate power to their owner. Again, the ways in which characters respond to these objects is revelatory of their spiritual condition. In *The Place of the Lion*, embodied Platonic archetypes in the form of massive animals serve as the objective focal point. In *Shadows of Ecstasy*, the "object" is both a person—an occult, charismatic, apparently immortal guru named Nigel Considine—and an idea—Considine's gospel of the transmutation of energies (cf. Newman 4). In *Descent into Hell*, the object is a play written by a modern-day Shakespeare. In *All Hallow's Eve*, it is a painting that appears to change as it reflects the psychological state of the novel's antagonist.

In *War in Heaven* and the Arthurian Poetry, the Holy Grail is the central sacral object—more precisely, several Hallows collectively serve this purpose, although the Grail is most prominent. "Hallows" are relics related to Christ, any physical items that are believed to have had contact with His physical body, or more specifically, items related to the Last Supper and the Crucifixion. The Grail is, then, merely the most famous of these objects throughout literary and Church history.

This kind of revelation-by-Hallows is, for instance, shown metonymically in "The Star of Percivale" (*Taliessin through Logres* 64-65), when members of Arthur's court gather to celebrate Mass:

> The household kneeled; the Lord Balin the Savage moved
> restless, through-thrust with a causeless vigil of anger;
> the king in the elevation beheld and loved himself crowned;
> Lancelot's gaze at the Host found only a ghost of the Queen (ll. 33-36).

Here, each person looks at the elements of the Lord's Supper—the bread, the wine—and sees instead of the Body of Christ his own object of idolatry. They pay dearly for this mortal sin: each suffers personal loss and grief, but—immeasurably worse—the very Kingdom of Logres is lost, and then follows the most dreadful catastrophe that could possibly befall the human race: "Against the rule of the Emperor the indivisible / Empire was divided; therefore the Parousia suspended / its coming, and abode still in the land of the Trinity" (145-47). The sins of Arthur and his kingdom postponed the second coming of Christ!

This idea of the revelatory sacral object is absolutely central to *The Chapel of the Thorn*, suggesting that it was one of Williams's earliest and most enduring ideas. The Hallow in this case is the Crown of Thorns forced upon Jesus' head by His executioners, now preserved in a tiny Chapel in some desolate southern corner of England. Throughout the play, with all its ambiguities, there is a hint of one moral message: misusing sacred objects reveals the damnation in one's heart.[24] This may be why Joachim hands over the Thorn, in the end, to his enemies without putting up a fight. It may be why the play ends with music, prayer, and praise (albeit to a variety of recipients), rather than with the battle that was brewing all along.

This is the same truth Williams continued to urge even in his last, greatest works: the crux of the Arthurian poetry has to do with use and abuse of the Grail and the power the Grail bestows. Arthur's great sin, in Williams's version, is his abuse of power, his abuse of his position as king over Logres, which is symbolically related to the Grail Hallows. At the moment of his crowning, Arthur asks himself, is "the king made for the kingdom, or the kingdom made for the king?" ("The Crowning of Arthur" in *Taliessin through Logres*, l. 63). This is the great question throughout Williams's mythology—and, indeed, his interpretation of life. The question is: Will I submit to my proper service, or will I insist on being served? It is apparent that King Arthur answers, "I will be served." This is comparable to Satan's "Better to reign in Hell, than serve in Heav'n" in *Paradise Lost* (Book I, line 263). Elizabeth Brewer writes: "For Williams, division comes about because Arthur has responded wrongly to the question as to whether the king exists for the kingdom, or the kingdom for the king, and in failing to identify himself with the kingdom, has brought disastrous consequences upon Logres" (Brewer 61). It is Arthur's selfish appropriation of power, resulting in (or from) indifference towards the Grail (McClatchey 108, 119), that destroys the kingdom.

The epigraph to *Taliessin through Logres* underscores the importance of human submission to office, which is frequently symbolized in Williams's poetry and fiction by a Hallow or other sacral object: "Unde est, quod non operatio propria propter essentiam, sed haec propter illam habet ut sit."[25] Arthur decided that the proper operation of the Kingdom existed for his sake, rather than vice-versa.

This sin is also committed in *Chapel*, by King Constantine. Constantine's last lines are deeply self-condemnatory in Williams's moral universe: "I shall be boasted over all old kings / Because I have set Christ above all gods" (II.658-59). Using Christ as a means to worldly fame is the worst kind of inversion of created order.

Affirmation and Negation

Throughout Church history, theologians, cloistered devotees, preachers, entire denominations, and ordinary Christians have struggled between two long-established, long-contested approaches to spirituality: the Affirmative Way (or *kataphatic* path) and the Negative Way (or *apophatic* path). These might be summarized by saying that someone on the path of the Affirmative Way to God uses all aspects of creation as ways to learn more about God, while a person on the Negative Way tries to separate him- or herself as far as possible from created things in order to experience God directly in His pure, unadulterated ontology. Williams defines these paths in *The Figure of Beatrice*:

> One, which is most familiar in records of sanctity, has been known as the Way of Rejection. It consists, generally speaking, in the renunciation of all images except the final one of God himself, and even—sometimes but not always—of the exclusion of that only Image of all human sense.... The other Way is the Way of Affirmation, the approach to God through these images (8-9).

The context makes clear that Williams includes all created objects in the category "images." Each of these two ways of approaching "images" has historical precedents, and each can claim Biblical authority. The Affirmative Way looks at passages such as Romans 1:20, which teaches that "God's invisible qualities—his eternal power and divine nature—have been clearly seen, being understood from what has been made." The Negative Way points to texts such as Isaiah 45:15, "Truly, You are a God who hides Himself" and images such as those in Psalm 97:2 in which "Clouds and thick darkness surround Him."

These two theologies are linguistic methods (ways of talking and writing about God), devotional practices (methods of prayer and meditation), and lifestyles (attitudes towards and specific practices of sexuality, aesthetics, culture, and community; cf. Carabine 8). Although each of the two Ways has had its adherents, "The proper celebration of the divinity requires that theology proceed both affirmatively and negatively" (Jones 19), and both are necessary for balanced Christian thought and life. Certainly "the two ways of seeking an understanding of God must admit that neither way can exclude the other" (Carabine 6). While scholars have tended to call him a proponent of the Way of Affirmation, Williams actually strove for a balance between the two, believing that neither was correct by itself, but needed the other as a constant corrective (see Ashenden's *Alchemy and Integration* on this point). I have argued elsewhere that, rather than achieving balance, Williams actually inter-implicated each Way with the other, destabilizing their differences in poetry and confusing their applications to daily Christian life (Higgins "Double Affirmation").

As might be expected, these two Ways struggle for dominance throughout *The Chapel of the Thorn*, too. More surprisingly, given that this play was written around the same time as *The Silver Stair*, a volume of negation, *Chapel* seems to fall—albeit very slightly—on the side of affirmation—as the discussion below of Romantic Theology should make clear. Yet it is a quieter, more restrained kind of affirmation than the extravagant erotic rituals Williams practiced and preached in his later years.

Romantic Theology

Williams's later doctrine of Romantic theology pervades these pages, in a bold form, although it is not clear whether the characters speak for Williams. In the following exchange, we learn that the villagers believe they have been taught Joachim that every love, every lust, every desire is a way towards God. They have a practice of buying female slaves as concubines, and have somehow come to think that this practice brings them closer to the divine. They are chastised by the Abbot, but there is no narrative voice to take sides in this debate, or any other.

> The Second VILLAGER: Joachim then lied,
> Teaching that God was in our midst and all
> Desire was from him and toward him at last?
> INNOCENT: Son, thou hast heard amiss.
> The Second VILLAGER: Mayhap. I heard
> Joachim teach that only a man's will
> Must be the rule and measure of his deed,
> That by his doing what he would to the height
> Should he find out the. . . God.
> INNOCENT: And if he taught
> That thou shouldst only work thy wicked will
> He taught a damnable heresy, as thou
> May'st find, in hell. (II:244-54).

Perhaps in this passage "Williams is showing up an obvious misunderstanding of his ... assertion of the mystical connections between erotic love and spiritual experience" (as Lindop argues in the preface to this volume, p. 2)—or perhaps he still misunderstood it himself.

Occult Imagery

Although *Chapel* was written in 1911-12 and William did not join the Fellowship of the Rosy Cross until 1917, magical or occult ideas are apparent in this play.[26] This suggests that he was reading deeply in hermetic texts long before he met A. E. Waite and joined a secret society.

For instance, the play starts out almost immediately with a pentagram: "While yet the candles be alight, go pray. / For these, or a five-cornered shape of stones / Frighten bad spirits further from men's tombs" (I:2-4). The pentagram or five-pointed star is a traditional occult symbol. As Lindop notes in the preface, p. 3 above, "Williams had probably encountered the 'five-cornered shape' of the pentagram, as a protection against evil spirits, in the pages of Eliphas Levi's *Mysteries of Magic*" (as translated by A. E. Waite). Williams makes a note about Levi on page 21 of the *Arthurian Commonplace Book*, discussing black Sabbath, cannibalism, child sacrifice, the magician's rod, and the golden sickle. There are references to A. E. Waite's book *The Hidden Church of the Holy Grail* in the *Commonplace Book*, on pages 37 and 70, and to "A E Waite's poems" on page 127. Of course, it is difficult to determine the date of individual entries in the *Commonplace Book*, so this is not solid proof that Williams had read Waite or Levi by 1912, but the use of occult symbols is suggestive.

The Hidden Church of the Holy Grail was published in 1909; this work by Waite had a strong influence on Williams. He continued to quote from it all the way until at least *The Figure of Arthur*, a work he left unfinished at his death (*Figure* 252; Brewer 56). Waite's ideas about the Grail were particularly significant: "*The Hidden Church of the Holy Graal* set out the history of the Grail legends and Waite's own distinctive interpretation of quasi-Gnostic strands that inform his whole approach to spirituality" (Ashenden 77), and Williams found these ideas essential for developing his own grail poetry:

> *The Hidden Church* later enabled Williams to reinterpret the story of the Grail for his own contemporaries in *War in Heaven, Taliessin Through Logres* and *The Region of the Summer Stars*…. it was this work which helped him to find in the Grail legend the perfect symbol-system for his insights into some aspects of the life of the spirit. (Brewer 55)

At the time he was writing *Chapel* and the *Commonplace Book*, Williams had not yet developed a systematic symbolic mythology. Yet his use of a sacred relic—the crown of thorns—shows that he was already thinking about how much symbolic weight an object could bear in poetry.

Waite also suggests in *The Hidden Church* that the Grail castle could be mapped on to the human body (Brewer 60); this, of course, is one of Williams's early sources for the anatomical geography he would use in the Arthurian poetry. There may perhaps be a hint of the nascent body-imagery in *Chapel*. In I:513, Innocent says that "The brain must teach and use the body," claiming that the Church is the brain, the world "the secular arm" (I:514). More specifically, there is a sense that the Crucifixion is going on simultaneously both in 33 A.D. and at the present moment in each Christian's body. Joachim entreats:

> Wilt thou do hurt? shall the hand smite the head?
> Shall thy foot bruise its fellow, wherethrough smote,
> Even as through thine, the nail that pierced the Christ,
> When all of us in Him were crucified? (I:356-59).

Our bodies are mapped onto Christ's in that quote. Similarly, when he finds that the villagers will not fight to defend the Thorn, Joachim asks:

> Know they not that this moment burns through time,
> God in his great aspect when all good things
> Shake on the verge of ruin, and Himself
> Hardly—yet wholly—wins with them through war?
> So once through Chaos, so on Calvary,
> So still, a flame within their inmost hearts,
> Against new usurpation of His rule? (II:383-89).

What happened at Creation happened again at the Crucifixion and is happening again in the very words, actions, and bodies of these characters. Finally, when Joachim gives up the Thorn, he accuses Innocent:

> His thought ye buffet, which He still allows,
> Enduring ever through the passionate world,
> That which on Calvary broke into our eyes. (II:597-99).

Again, there is that simultaneity of all times and the patterning of our bodies according to their identification with Christ's.

There are a few other hermetic echoes in this play, too. One of them is the concept of a secret, magical name. In I:623-24, Amael says that he is "A priest in mine own office" who has "a name therein that none may speak." The idea of "As above, so below" also informs *Chapel*'s mysticism. This is the principle of correspondence, or of the microcosm and the macrocosm, as described in *The Emerald Tablet of Hermes*. One of its tenets (in Madame Blavatsky's translation) is "What is below is like that which is above, and what is above is similar to that which is below to accomplish the wonders of the one thing." This principle is subtly operative throughout many of Williams's works and is clearly referenced in these lines, when Gregory says about Innocent:

>   I have heard him say,
> Preaching before the king upon a feast,
> That, since God acts not many times but once
> For ever, when he —thou hast heard their tale—
> Worked wood in Nazareth, to those who saw
> Dust-fashioned he to stars and clay to men,
> Wherein all those who labour have their part:
> This I remember for that afterwards
> Old Andreas the carpenter, who died,
> Laughed at his toil, swearing he made the worlds. (II:361-70).

This passage gathers together the theme of the simultaneity of all times ("God acts not many times but once / For ever") with the idea that the local carpenter's work is a microcosm of God's creative work throughout the whole universe. It is worth keeping these ideas in mind while reading this play and then moving on into Williams's later works.

The Taliessin Poems

A comparison to the late Arthurian poetry (*Taliessin through Logres*, 1938, and *The Region of the Summer Stars*, 1944) and to the mature dramas (especially *The House of the Octopus*, 1945) is in some ways unfruitful. Such a comparison reveals the inadequacies of Williams's early style, but taking *Chapel* on its own terms is an enjoyable and rewarding exercise.

Williams's prosody changed drastically after 1930, when he edited the poems of Gerard Manley Hopkins (Cavaliero 98, Dunning 112, Higgins and Talbot 64). His meter became faster, less regular, and more original. He learned how to handle the sentence against the line with more aplomb. His diction lost most of its stilted archaisms. For instance, read these lines from one of Amael's powerful speeches in *Chapel*:

> I know the forest-paths, I know the caves
> Whence the first men crawled, with lean hands that clawed
> Like the wild beasts they learned their hunting from!
> I know the smell of blood upon the track
> Where first men snarled above the prey 'lo, mine!'
> I know the wantonness in women's eyes,
> The lust of cruelty in their masters' hands,
> And all the treacheries of the warring worlds!
> I have gone down and in a dark night laid
> My hands upon the leash of that desire

> Which evermore the gods let loose on us,
> And felt about my brows the wind-like lust
> That blows to changing shapes this mist of men! (II:278-90).

Now compare those with the beginning of "Taliessin's Song of the Unicorn" from *Taliessin through Logres*:

> Shouldering shapes of the skies of Broceliande
> are rumours in the flesh of Caucasia; they raid the west,
> clattering with shining hooves, in myth scanned—
> centaur, gryphon, but lordlier for verse is the crest
> of the unicorn, the quick panting unicorn; he will come
> to a girl's crooked finger or the sharp smell
> of her clear flesh—but to her no good; the strum
> of her blood takes no riot or quiet from the quell;
> she cannot like such a snorting alien love (ll.1-9).

The entire thirty-six-line unicorn poem is one virtuosic sentence. Notice that both are in iambic pentameter, but that the later poem takes many more liberties with metrical substitutions and inversions. Amael's speech is much more strongly monosyllabic and end-stopped, while Taliessin's is heavily enjambed and employs a Latinate, polysyllabic, mythic diction. The syntax of the later poem is more complex: each of Amael's sentences begins with a straight-forward subject-predicate combination.[27] Taliessin's single-sentence song begins with a subject separated from its predicate by a prepositional phrase, giving a sense of delay and complication to the action. The later selection is arguably more difficult to understand, but also creates its own atmosphere or "kappa element"[28] by means of its techniques.

In addition to the great improvements to his verse that Williams gained by editing Hopkins's poems, he also enjoyed wider experience with theatrical writing throughout his life. Reading through his plays in chronological order reveals growing technical prowess and insight into how to convey spiritual drama on the stage. A comparison between Chapel, his first play, and *House of the Octopus*, his last completed stage play, does emphasize the profound depth of his later ability. Yet *Chapel* stands up surprisingly well to this late work. The lines of poetry in 1912 are clean, clear, and dramatic. They have good auditory quality. The characters live on the stage.

Indeed, the two plays—his first and last—have some elements in common. Both employ the so-called Aristotelian unities: of time, place, and action. Each is set in a limited area outside a Chapel, within a short span of time (apparently one day), and focus on one specific crisis or conflict. In *Chapel*, the conflict is over possession of the Thorn and its Chapel. In *House of the Octopus*, the crisis is a question of compromise vs. martyrdom: will the missionary, Anthony, and his young Christians face death, or will they say that their God has the same name as the evil Emperor of P'o-l'u? Each is a drama of spiritual loyalties and metaphysical realities acted out in the deeds of the characters. Each is a powerful piece of theater, and it is to be hoped that both see the stage again soon and often.

TEXTUAL NOTES

In transcribing this work and preparing it for publication, some editorial decisions were required when handwriting or revisions made points unclear. These are generally discussed in the endnotes. I have decided to retain Williams's nonstandard punctuation in places, most notably when he uses a dash combined with other marks, but have silently corrected instances of two dots to a standard ellipsis. I believe that retaining some peculiarities brings the reader closer to Williams without any concomitant loss of clarity. I have very rarely made a small silent correction to other punctuation, such as adding a comma for clarity. It appears that Williams underlined text that he wanted to have set in italics, but was not always consistent on this point. I have occasionally standardized italicization for clarity and have formatted stage directions slightly differently than they appear in the manuscript. All other matters are covered in the endnotes.

ACKNOWLEDGEMENTS

Although *The Chapel of the Thorn* is a short play, written by one man over 100 years ago, many people were involved in its inspiration, writing, editing, revision, transcription, interpretation, and preparation for publication. As the introductory essay makes clear, even the independent and charismatic "CW" sought the advice of friends as he worked on this little drama. How much more, then, must the editor of the present edition beg mercy in the inadequate expression of her gratitude.

Thanks are due to Georgia Glover of David Higham Associates of London, Julia Masnik of Watkins-Loomis Agency, and Bruce Hunter of the Charles Williams Estate for permission to publish this text.

The past and present staff of the Marion E. Wade Center—Chris Mitchell, Marjorie Lamp Mead, Laura Schmidt, Heidi Truty, Shawn Mrakovich, and Kendra Juskus—have succeeded in making that jewel of an archive into a tiny unfallen Eden on earth. I must thank them particularly for hunting down obscure references, making materials ready for my visits, and providing both friendly hospitality and professional research services. I would like to note here my grief at Chris Mitchell's passing, which occurred during the preparation of this book.

Several scholars have contributed their efforts to the present edition. Clearly, I would have achieved little without Grevel Lindop and David Llewellyn Dodds, whose original and ground-breaking work is included as preface and appendix, respectively, and whom I cite profusely. They each also provided me with other documents, including extracts from Lindop's forthcoming biography *Charles Williams: The Last Magician*, and the entirety of Dodds's introductory essay to Williams's *Arthurian Commonplace Book*. David also sent me a chronology of Williams's correspondence with Pellow, and stayed up all one night scanning the pages of the *Arthurian Commonplace Book* and emailing them to me (following permission from the CW Estate, of course). I thank these gentlemen for sharing their work with me and with our readers. I am honored to be in their company on these pages.

Grevel and David also read and commented on my introductory essay in draft, as did Brenton Dickieson. Brenton also spent time in the Wade checking the accuracy of my typescript, and Brandon Wold and Katie Clark did as well. Brandon, especially, worked hard as my research assistant. Richard Sturch looked up references in the catalog of the Charles Williams Society Library for me, and Judith

Priestman did the same at the Bodleian. Charles Franklyn Beach provided me with some Williams materials; he and Gavin Ashenden both checked references. Andrew Lazo hunted down the source (and a translation) of the Latin hymn at the end of the play, and Richard Sturch provided his own prose translation. Other friends and associates on social media provided lively, intelligent conversations on the Latin and other points related to Charles Williams's life and works.

In addition to the encouragement and support of scholars, I have also been cheered on by friends and family while preparing this project. A huge thank-you goes to Rebecca Tirrell Talbot for hosting me while I commuted from her apartment in Chicago to the Wade. Cheers to Dominic Christison, James Femister, Elizabeth Gahman, Sharon Gerdes, Jeffrey Harvey, Joshua Lazarus, Andrew Stirling MacDonald, and Nick Muth for giving *The Chapel of the Thorn* its debut reading at a meeting of Ekphrasis: Fellowship of Christians in the Arts. Thanks to my sister Eve for reading and listening to the entire play while we checked for errors. And lots of love to Gary and all my family for their enthusiasm. It is a great blessing to be surrounded by those who are as crazy as I am about (or at least indulge my madness for) the oddest Inkling.

—Sørina Higgins

---

[1] This quote is found on page 41 of Hallowell's *Modern Canterbury Pilgrims*, but can also be found in many books discussing either Auden or the Inklings, such as Humphrey Carpenter's *The Inklings* or his biography of Auden, Alan Jacobs's *The Narnian*, and Edward Mendelson's *Later Auden*.

[2] The fullest account to date of Williams's biography is Alice Hadfield's *Charles Williams: An Exploration*. Grevel Lindop has recently completed his biography (from which the preface to this edition of *Chapel* is drawn), entitled *Charles Williams: The Last Magician*, to be published by Oxford University Press in 2015.

[3] For an account of Williams's activities in the F∴R∴C∴ and other useful background information on A. E. Waite and the 20th-century English Rosicrucians, refer to R. A. Gilbert's *A. E. Waite: Magician of Many Parts* and *The Golden Dawn: Twilight of the Magicians*; Gavin Ashenden's *Charles Williams: Alchemy and Integration*; Ellic Howe's *The Magicians of the Golden Dawn*; and Gareth Knight's *The Magical World of the Inklings*.

[4] CW / MS-113 in the Wade Center.

[5] David Llewellyn Dodds has written, so far as the editor can determine, the only published article about *Chapel*—and the editor is happy to be able to include it as an appendix to this volume. Much of this chronological information is taken from that article.

[6] In his unpublished biography of Charles Williams, *The Last Magician*, and in the preface to this volume, which is drawn from that work.

[7] The date written on the manuscript held by the Wade reads "C.W. Aug 24/12."

[8] The editor would like to thank her research assistant at the Marion E. Wade Center, Brandon Wold, for cross-checking deductions on drafts and many other points.

[9] If Williams actually finished the play in 1924, this must mean that he revised it heavily in that year. In that case, the MS from 1912 in the Wade, from which this edition was transcribed, is not his "latest intention," and the final version is lost. Here is one more wild suggestion: Is it possible that he finished the *first draft* of the play in May of 1924, and then that "Aug 24/12" written on the MS means Augsut 12th, 1924? This seems unlikely.

[10] Grand Rapids: Eerdmans, 1990.

[11] A note in Raymond Hunt's hand on the MS, p. 2, reads "Received from Charles Williams (via Miss Margaret Douglas) by registered post from Oxford, on the morning of 1st April 1942."

[12] David Dodds suggests that the Constantine in the play is, indeed, the Great, and also offers possible historical identifications for Innocent and Joachim; see the Appendix, p. 125.

[13] Of course, since the play is interested in a drama of ideas, all the characters are somewhat symbolic, with varying degrees of credibility, authenticity, and depth. On this point, which is a criticism often made of Williams's novels, see the article "Is a 'Christian' Mystery Story Possible? Charles Williams' *War in Heaven* as a Generic Case Study," by the editor of this edition.

[14] On this topic, consider the following works. D. T. Myers, "Brave New World: The Status of Women According to Tolkien, Lewis and Williams," *Cimmaron Review* 17 (1971): 13-19. Amy Nyman, "Feminist Perspective in Williams' Novels," *Mythlore* 12.4 (1986): 3-9. Lisa Hopkins, "Female Authority Figures in the Works of Tolkien, C. S. Lewis, and Charles Williams," *Mythlore* 20:4 (1995): 364-366. Sam McBride and Candice Fredrick, *Women Among the Inklings: Gender, C. S. Lewis, J. R. R. Tolkien, and Charles Williams* (Praeger, 2001).

[15] Andrea Freud Loewenstein has written just such a study of both these issues, entitled *Loathsome Jews and Engulfing Women* (New York University Press, 1993), but a contrasting study is still needed, as hers suffers from serious flaws; see, for instance, David Dodds's review in the Charles Williams Society *Newsletter* 75 (1994): 6-10. As an alternative, the editor recommends "The Gendered Body in Charles Williams" by Andrew Rasmussen in the forthcoming volume *The Inklings and King Arthur*.

[16] The exact date of composition for *The Silver Stair* is not known: Williams presented the manuscript to his future wife, Florence Conway, in January of 1909 or 1910, probably 1910 (Hadfield *Exploration* 16).

[17] These sentences will sound quite ironic if it turns out that *Chapel* was written in 1924.

[18] On this point, see (for example) the chapter entitled "History's Words" in Lewis's *The Pilgrim's Regress* (145-150), Lewis's *Surprised by Joy* 235, Lewis's *Letters* II:35, Lewis's essay "Myth Became Fact," Tolkien's poem "Mythopoeia" (readily found online), and Tolkien's essay "On Fairy-Stories."

[19] On this point, the editor recommends Richard Sturch's article "Charles Williams as Heretic?" in the *Charles Williams Quarterly* 136 (2010): 7-19.

[20] The *Commonplace Book* is kept in Oxford University's Bodeian Library; unfortunately, the Marion E. Wade Center does not have a copy. The editor has access to this work by the extreme generosity of Williams scholar David Llewellyn Dodds, who shared both the text of the *Commonplace Book* and his own highly intelligent introductory essay and exhaustive notes. He has taken the time to track down the source of nearly every quote or reference in his MS: a labor of much time and very great love and care. For more discussion of the *Commonplace Book*, see Dodds's appendix below, pp. 124, 125, 135-6.

[21] This story is fictionalized and dramatized in the excellent graphic novel *Heaven's War*, which also imagines Williams exchanging his life for C. S. Lewis's.

[22] The editor's thanks are due to Grevel Lindop for pointing out these instances.

[23] See also Dodds, p. 131 below.

[24] See also Dodds, p. 135, 136 below.

[25] This is from Dante's *De Monarchia* I:111. Williams's own translation is: 'The proper operation (working or function) is not in existence for the sake of the being, but the being for the sake of the operation' (*The Figure of Beatrice*, 40). He also paraphrases it in *The Descent of the Dove* as "the essence is created for the sake of the function and not the function for the essence" (132).

[26] See also the preface, p. 3 above.

[27] Except for "I have gone down and in a dark night laid…." And even that begins with a simple subject-verb combination, but then the second verb of the predicate is postponed by a prepositional phrase.

[28] Lewis, C. S. "On Stories," which was originally given as a talk called "The Kappa Element in Literature"; cf. Ward, *Planet Narnia*, 15.

THE CHAPEL OF THE THORN:
A DRAMATIC POEM

"Think not that I am come to send peace on earth:
I come not to send peace but a sword…
a man's foes shall be they of his own household."
Matthew 10:34, 36

Dramatis Personae

The King CONSTANTINE

THEODORIC a lord

INNOCENT Abbot of the Monastery of St. Cyprian

Prior JOHN

JOACHIM Priest of the Chapel of the Holy Thorn

MICHAEL acolyte at the Chapel

AMAEL a singer and priest of Druhild

GREGORY the headman of the village

Men and Women of the village and township; Monks; Forest-men; Lords, Spearmen, and others of the King's train.

Setting

The Chapel of the Holy Thorn is built between the high-road and the edge of a sea-cliff. To the southward this road descends to a fishing-village on the lower shore; to the northward it follows the curve of the coast as far as the capital city. In front of the Chapel two other paths also meet; one, from the north-west, comes directly through the hills from the capital; the other, from the south-west, connects the Chapel with the newly-built monastery of Saint Cyprian. In the open space at the meeting of these four roads the action of the poem takes place. The ground is steep and rough; beyond the Chapel, which is an old and small building, can be seen the edge of the cliff. The sound of the sea is continually heard.

The first act passes in the late afternoon on the vigil of the feast of St. Cyprian; the second in the morning of the feast. The weather is dull and stormy.

Act I

[*A WOMAN and two MEN
of the village are standing in
front of the Chapel.*

The First MAN: Take heed, lest evil things be come abroad.

The Second MAN: While yet the candles be alight, go pray.
                              For these, or a five-cornered shape of stones
                              Keep bad spirits far from men's tombs.

The First MAN: Go swiftly, ere the priest sing to an end,   5
                              If thou canst hope aught helpful from his god.

The WOMAN: My mother came, and I come.

The First MAN: Well, good chance
                              Be with thy prayers!

The Second MAN: May the white Christ-lord lay
                              Spells on the wood-witch till she heal thy son.

The WOMAN: He had a mother.
                                              [*She goes in to the Chapel.*

The Second MAN: Will her son live?

The First MAN: No: 10
                              My mother's father in such sickness died
                              On the ninth day.

The Second MAN: What, is it pestilence?

The First MAN: No, for six nights of eight I slept with him,
                              Taking no harm, but when the plague was full,
                              It slew both Andreas and his chamber-maid   15
                              In a night and day-dawn: this is not the plague…
                              By token that I thought to buy the wench,
                              Later, if he grew willing; fair, small-boned,
                              Clean-skinned, not much a talker, diligent.

The Second MAN:	They who work now about the convent hear	20
	This sale betwixt ourselves of chamber-maids	
	Is frowned on, and shall soon be brought to end.	

The First MAN: What, must a man be bound in to his wife,
To wrangling lips, and hard, lean arms and hands?
Out on them!

The Second MAN: Priests' thought! they that have no wives   25
Know not what thing 'tis to keep house with one.
When comes your toll of labour round once more?

The First MAN: Too soon, a seven-night hence. I have a mind
To sell my maid (lusty she is and young)
For a crown and that work done on my behoof.   30

The Second MAN: Give also a mess at evening after work,
And we would talk of bargaining.

                              [*GREGORY comes in from the town-road.*

GREGORY: Well-met,
Brothers: are ye bent town-ward?

The First MAN: Aye; and thou?

GREGORY: Hither I come to speak with Joachim,
For in the town is rumour that this day,   35
Or morrow—on Saint Cyprian's day—at last
Will the Lord Abbot seize by force the Thorn,
And set monks in this Chapel.

The First MAN: For the Thorn,
What care have we for that? but for this land,
It is the tomb of Druhild of the Trees.—   40

The Second MAN: By the hight of Druhild, none shall wall it round.

The First MAN: For this our fathers came to watch these priests,
This Joachim and his like, since Cyprian first
Built over the tomb an altar to his god.

GREGORY: Aye. Well, let be. To-morrow or to-night, 45
Joachim first to me, then I to you,
And ye to all our village-men give word.
They cannot build walls in a single sun.

[*The two men go out:* MICHAEL
comes down from the Chapel.]

Hail, Michael!

MICHAEL: Hail, Gregory!

GREGORY: Why, lad,
Where is thy *benedicite*? be sure 50
Thou hadst it prompt enough upon thy tongue
When first thou hadst thy lesson. Hast forgot?

MICHAEL: No.

GREGORY: Must I speak then—benedicite?

MICHAEL: Benedicite! pax tecum Domini!

GREGORY: Where is the priest?

MICHAEL: In the Chapel! where else, he? 55

GREGORY: How long in the Chapel shall he watch the Thorn?

MICHAEL: Till my lord Abbot take it. Well, good speed
Hasten the hands of my lord Abbot then!

GREGORY: Art thou old Joachim's acolyte, to speak
Thus? thou wilt yield the Thorn up, and not fight? 60

MICHAEL: Fight! will the village-men dare fight the monks?
Joachim is too old, but I will fight!
I will fight—I will not fast and watch the Thorn.
For I am weary of these prayers and hymns
And mysteries of the holy bread and wine, 65
And spiritual visions to be seen
In due time, if I fast and watch the Thorn!

| GREGORY: | Nay, how wilt thou in after-years endure
To keep this place when Joachim is dead,
If thereof thou be weary even now? | 70 |

| MICHAEL: | I will not be a priest: better it were
To be a trapper, herdsman, fisherman,
Or else a shipman. Gregory, how oft
Hast thou gone over the sea to cities? |

| GREGORY: | Once. |

| MICHAEL: | Once! and this father Joachim not at all!—
Blessed saints! What have these old men done with life? | 75 |

| GREGORY: | Yea so? What matter have those lands to show? |

| MICHAEL: | What matter? what to show? All men and things!
Ports where a thousand ships may ride at ease,
And markets of sweet perfumes; images,
White stone and purple,—iron-caged animals,
Flat scaly fish as long as thirty spears,
Lions caught in the desert,—sun-stained palaces
Whose stairs are lit as if upon each wall
Innumerable altar-candles burned,—
Kings who have black men for their cup-bearers,
And yellow-featured slant-eyed slaves for guard,
And twisted crowns cut from a single jewel,
And swords graved thick with spells of warlocks dead,
And broideries so rich—all men! all things! …
It is thy brother's son himself whose tales
Are all about this shore, and even here
Were told when he brought offering to the Thorn.
Hast thou heard nothing? | 80

85

90 |

| GREGORY: | Aye, aye: he is young.
Nevertheless, thou yet shalt be a priest
In spite of him or my lord Abbot. | 95 |

| MICHAEL: | Priest! …
What like were they who were the priests of old
Long ere the blessed Cyprian brought the Thorn
Over the sea and drove them out? |

GREGORY:	He? Nay,	
	Those priests fled not for Cyprian or his Thorn	100
	(Albeit it was about the white Christ's brows	
	When he was slain):— naught but the king's decree	
	And all the land being wrathful in the fear	
	Of famine, drove them hence. Nor thou shalt be	
	As the least among those strong-limbed boys who stood—	105

[*AMAEL descends from the hill-path.*

AMAEL: Hail, Gregory!

GREGORY: Amael?

AMAEL: Hail, in the name of the gods!
Or even by now have ye forgot the gods?

GREGORY: Why hast thou come hither? there be still
Edicts put forth against all singers, bards,
Minstrels, and priests of ancient things. Get hence.   110

AMAEL: The ships of Gorlias wait yet seven days
Ere they and I go south; in which space I,
Last singer and high-priest of this land's gods,
Walk through the land once more; for I have dwelled
Amid the Western peoples till your king   115
Came with the Cross-banner, and all his host,—
And on a day their last bedizened chief
Stood up beyond his city, in the hills,
all his house and bards were slain, and he
Even while his sword swung over Constantine.   120

GREGORY: Are then thy gods so utterly cast down?
It is no long time since those Western lords
Held Constantine to tribute.

AMAEL: Nay, the gods
Change not until the worlds be wrecked, but now
Are angry with their servants.

GREGORY:	If it be,	125
	Linger a little, secretly, hard by,	
	And thou shalt yet perchance behold a thing	
	To make a last song—yea, perchance thyself	
	Shalt do a work that other bards may sing.	

AMAEL: What wilt thou do? wilt thou burn up the Thorn? 130
If still that sign of the white Christ be kept
As ere the bards were driven forth.

GREGORY: 'Tis here.
I go to warn the dwellers by the shore
That my lord Abbot (he that drave thee forth)
Gathers the king's men: needs we all must fight 135
Who were content to watch and wait, till now
This Abbot needs must seize and build a wall
(Being jealous of the old man Joachim)
About this plot, till none shall more go in,
Or point, saying 'So, the tomb of Druhild!'—

AMAEL: Gods! 140
Avenge yourselves!

MICHAEL: And therefore will ye fight…
But Joachim deems you zealous for God's Thorn!

GREGORY: Ah, boy, the heroes of this land are dead
Unto King Constantine, their names forgot,
Save if a man dare speak them he is slain… 145
But we are from their land, their race, their kind:
Let Joachim keep his Thorn, and let the monks
Plead, plot, or fight to gain it from him. We
Fight for the tomb of Druhild of the Trees.

AMAEL: Ye do well. Let the people, the poor folk, 150
Bow down their heads indeed, before the Cross,
But in their hearts remember as they will.
Keeps Joachim still the wardship of the Thorn?

GREGORY: Aye, with young Michael here for acolyte.

AMAEL: Grows he not old?

GREGORY:	Aye, with a greater weight	155

          Than all his days upon him, for he bears
          The times of twain his brethren, they who died
          In the great plague, last followers of his creed.

AMAEL: Do his eyes grow more dim that theirs are shut,
          Or his limbs weaken because theirs are still?   160

GREGORY: Nay, yet their hands pluck at him from their grave.

AMAEL: How many years have passed since they two died?
          Eight?

GREGORY: Seven.

AMAEL: Seven, by a sign. There fell
          Since then each year a trial upon the land,
          For first there blew the pestilence, and then   165
          Famine—albeit there were but few to feed—
          And the third year the king went forth to war,
          And warred three years more; and for twelve months since
          Hath built a convent for his thanks to God.

MICHAEL: That is the white Christ… who hath given him power.   170

AMAEL: This man hath served your white Christ long enough.
          How lacked the king an earlier triumph?

GREGORY: He!
          What hath this man to do with kings or wars?
          But when there came new men across the sea,
          Clerks, and men learnèd in scriptures, and high-priests   175
          Prouder than lords, these overbore the king;
          Who therefore left his father's gods, and then
          Stood underneath new altars with new vows,
          At the word of Innocent drove forth the bards,
          Fought, and won battle over rebels and foes,   180
          And now builds convents.

AMAEL: Are these things to you
          Aught?

GREGORY: Save that we grow poorer, …hunger, plague,
War, tax of labour; that these new laws be
Burden, and steal a man's will from his hearth,
And leave him no peace in his house-life, naught. 185
But always we remember the old kings, …
Heroes, …and Druhild, master of our folk.

AMAEL: It is a great thing: yet, O Gregory,
These heroes are not as the immortal gods,
Under whose might our fathers wrought of old, 190
And made their name to seaward as a sword
And as a fire to landward, they whose names
May not be uttered save of us, their priests,
Over the bloody sacrificial stone:—
Have men forgotten? will they fight for tombs, 195
And will not fight or dare at all for gods?
Look, I will lay enchantment on their spears,
Strengthen their arms with magic, make the hearts
Of the king's host as poison to the blood,—
Call them to battle for the ancient things! 200

GREGORY: Nay, but we know not: we are dull to learn,
And in our days have worshipped many gods,
Worshipped the old and new, for need it is
A man should have a god's name in his mouth
To pray to or to swear by or for fight; 205
And as the kings turn must the peasants turn.
But wheresoever we bow down or no,
Yea, though we bow down or we bow not down,
Still are we hungered when the harvest fails,
Thirsty with labour, sun-burnt, chill with rain. 210
Gods change, and we: yet little is to change.
This changes not, men eat and work and sleep,
Have women, die; and always, over all,
Good skies or evil, …if these be the gods.

MICHAEL: Ah, surely there be other gods than Time! 215

GREGORY: Many names hath Time to youth, and few to age:
But always he is one through length of years
In equal rising and setting of the sun.
Mayhap there be more gods: I cannot tell.

MICHAEL:	Are this man then and Joachim—He comes!	220

                                                                   [*Two or three women go from the Chapel toward the village. JOACHIM comes out.*

JOACHIM: God's peace be with you, brethren!

GREGORY: Father, Hail!

AMAEL: Hail, servant of God crucified!

GREGORY [*apart to AMAEL*]:   Be still!
Wilt thou bring ruin on thyself and us?

JOACHIM: Ah, voice of mine enemy! Art thou returned,
O Amael? whence and wherefore art thou come?   225

AMAEL: From going up and down through other lands,
From hearing other speech in alien huts
Or wild beasts' tread in darkness beyond fires.

JOACHIM: O Amael, to what purpose comest thou?

AMAEL: I come to count up all who yet have gained   230
Right wages for their duty toward thy god,
To sing a last song unto mind.

JOACHIM: What gifts
Herein shall satisfy thy heart for them?
Ask Gregory if they again desire
The ancient worship and the ways of old!   235

AMAEL: Hear'st thou, O Gregory? answer: what hath Christ
Brought thee that none among the old gods gave?

GREGORY: New laws in new compulsion on our lives.

AMAEL: But what word speaks he more than they would speak?

GREGORY: A word of preaching, and a word of sin,   240
Of terror, and denial, and unrest
In all our hearts for all we think or do.

The Chapel of the Thorn

JOACHIM: But out of such heart-Golgotha of pain
Springs there no fount of him in pardon, sweet
To skull-shaped hills of life?

GREGORY: Truly, yet we
Knew naught of sin or pardon till he came. 245

JOACHIM: He came? long time this Chapel hath been here,
And men to teach him.

GREGORY: *Thou* hast for long time
Dwelt here, but what part hast thou in the talk
Of Abbots, monks, and king's priests?

JOACHIM: Yet all we 250
Teach the Lord Christ.

GREGORY: Who of us fears thy Christ?

JOACHIM: It is not well that any man should fear
Christ, till his will be won into desire.
No man may fear God save as lovers fear.

AMAEL: I also teach desire, my brother.

JOACHIM: Thou? 255

AMAEL: Women for love, vengeance for hate: what more?

JOACHIM: Thy word is but a twilight, Amael.
Such loves and hates are as the firstling flames
Which crackle through life when the torch of birth
Quickens a man's will into fire for God. 260

AMAEL: O sun of knowledge, certainty of noon!
And yet methinks but now I heard some tale
How many of thy brethren strive with thee!
Christ's servants hot in wrangling o'er Christ's tomb.

JOACHIM: Thou that hast not begun to learn of Christ, 265
How canst thou tell what wars hide in his name?
Nevertheless, thou hast said truly. Once

	The swords and spears fashioned this crown of old,	
	And now would take it to themselves again:	
	The priest hath kissed the soldier. Gregory,	270
	What say the village-men?	

GREGORY: Well-bent are they
To keep this Chapel's treasure for their own,
Even as far as to the strife of swords.

JOACHIM: They fight for their own souls, which while they do
To none on earth will I give up the Thorn,   275
Nor to the king-robed, king-crowned Abbot yield
That symbol of man's freedom and God's love,—
While those who fight, and these young lads wait to guard
The Crown when I shall perish. Wilt thou fight
For thy succession, Michael?

MICHAEL: For aught,   280
Rather than lose myself in prayers again!

                                          [*The Prior JOHN enters from
                                          the convent path.*

JOHN: Benedicite, my children!

AMAEL [*apart to GREGORY*]:   Who is this?

GREGORY [*apart to AMAEL*]:
Next in his office to the Abbot, Prior.

JOHN: I come to Joachim, servant of the Thorn.

JOACHIM: Prior John, I hear thee: speak.

JOHN: Thus saith my lord: 285
Wilt thou be still a scandal, an offense,
A rock of stumbling in the path of souls,
An act of disobedience, an ill thought
In the shaft of God and our authority—?

JOACHIM: Get to the matter: what is thy desire?   290

JOHN: To-morrow is Saint Cyprian's day.—Repent;
Splinter no more the Church's unity;
With visions and wild words deceive no more
This land: submit, yield us the relic!

JOACHIM: Where
Is any cause for such deed?

JOHN: Is it thine 295
To seek for causes when my lord commands?

JOACHIM: Yet surely some good reason moves his will.

JOHN: This house is hidden in a narrow place,
Hard and obscure to pilgrims is the way.

JOACHIM: Must pilgrimage be made an easy thing? 300

JOHN: What if this Chapel were attacked by thieves?

JOACHIM: What band of thieves should steal a growth of thorn?

JOHN: Nay, but the gifts that the religious bring—

JOACHIM: What matter those, so but the Thorn remain?

JOHN: Surely such dear Remembrance should be kept 305
With ritual, with incessant guard of prayer,
And all the sacred watch of holy Church.

JOACHIM: Fully in one devout heart is the Church
Manifest, as in worship of a realm.

JOHN: Doubtless thine own heart in thy thought outweighs 310
All worth of ceremonial; thou art he,
Solely, hast holiness to guard the Thorn.

JOACHIM: For mine oath's sake and Cyprian's name I keep
This relic once delivered; thence apart,
Not mine own self nor any dare I weigh. 315
In each man's separate being God is judge;
Therein his will's indictment and reward.

JOHN:	Thine obstinacy shall obtain reward	
	On the last day, when He descends to judge;	
	Unless to-day, before the king come down,	320
	Thy soul be humbled to give up the Thorn.	

MICHAEL: Though the king come, the Abbot, and the monks,
And though their battle rage with spears and psalms,
I and my father will possess the Thorn.

JOHN: Ere many days be closed shalt thou be set   325
Such penance,—

MICHAEL: What, by bald-heads that would spend
Their slow hours, nodding underneath the Thorn?

JOACHIM: Peace, Michael: this is grown too great a time
For thee to know it; thee, or this Prior John.

MICHAEL [*half-apart*]:
Peace, peace! but not from prayers or psalms or hymns.   330

AMAEL: Well has thou said, and as a high king. Come,
We twain will speak of such kings.—

                              [*A* MAN *runs in.*

The MAN: Sanctuary!

JOHN [*simultaneously with* JOACHIM, *below*]:
Go to the altar in the Chapel, son!

JOACHIM [*simultaneously with* JOHN, *above*]:
Brother, what trouble haunts thee to such haste?

The MAN: By devil's spite my arrow slew but now   335
My lord's horse as he rode: death hunts me down.

JOACHIM: Who is thy lord?

The MAN: Theodoric.

GREGORY: Nay then,
If he be following, death is at thy heel.

JOHN:	Into the Chapel, into the Chapel, fool!	
JOACHIM:	I cannot think... aye, go in, friend... No man
Should slay man for such cause.	340

[*The MAN goes into the Chapel.*

JOHN: Thou know'st as much
As thou has seen in vision, little more.

AMAEL [*apart to GREGORY*]:
          Which of these men shall fight Theodoric?
          Better he fled along the village road,—
          There might at need be hiding,—

GREGORY [*apart to AMAEL*]:   Should our huts   345
          For but this man's sake burn and we be slain?

[*THEODORIC and his forest-men rush up.*

THEODORIC: Up to the chapel! there he hides!

JOACHIM [*between the men and the Chapel*]:   What haste,
          Brethren, upon what errand speeds your feet?

THEODORIC:	Thrust him aside and enter! Back, old man!
Or rather, tell us if one came but now
Running for shelter?	350
JOHN:	No.	
JOACHIM:	If—	

THEODORIC: Go ye in!
          Stand thou aside to see my will with him!

JOACHIM: Nay, but except for God's sake none go in
          With arms before the altar of the Thorn.

THEODORIC:	Short time shall aught prevent my axes. On!	355

JOACHIM: Wilt thou do hurt? shall the hand smite the head?
Shall thy foot bruise its fellow, wherethrough smote,
Even as through thine, the nail that pierced the Christ,
When all of us in Him were crucified?—

THEODORIC: Thou and thy Christ! is this a time for words? 360
Give back!

> [*As he seizes JOACHIM, the Abbot INNOCENT comes swiftly up the village-path and thrusts himself between. MONKS follow by twos and threes.*]

INNOCENT: Who dare lay hand upon a priest?
Who dare go up on armed feet against God?

THEODORIC: A villain slew my horse and hides himself
Yonder from me.

INNOCENT: He then is surely housed
From temporal hands and secular arrest. 365

THEODORIC: Housed! and what justice hast thou for my cause?

INNOCENT: We hold an inquisition three days hence
Into all causes whereof an appeal
By high or low is to our justice made.
There come. 370

THEODORIC: Shall I be called to stand among the churls
Of yonder village, trial on trial, until
It please thy pomp of abbacy to hear
A forest-carle against me? By God's Face,
This man is mine and shall be seized now!

INNOCENT: Thine? 375
Lord, learn thou hast no spearman, gateman, page,
…What say we? …wife, child, if our lips forbid

The Chapel of the Thorn 57

      In name of the Church their service. He thy man?
      If thou set foot or speak word more than we
      Allow thee, at due time, damned art thou—damned!   380
      Thy man—at the altar?
      Ho, children, go in: bring this man forth!
                   So.
      Circle him round! raise the Magnificat…
      Deposuit! …
            how seize him, lord: that hour
      The curse of God and of His Mother frees   385
      Thy men (thy men!—) from their allegiance, bars
      All converse with thee, gives thy lands and holds
      To any who will serve the Church, thy soul
      To the devil, his angels, and the seven sins!
      On, children!

                 [*The King* CONSTANTINE
                 enters, followed by his LORDS,
                 by SPEARMEN *and*
                 VILLAGERS. *The* MONKS *go*
                 out with the fugitive.]

AMAEL: For thy land or for thy soul   390
      Art thou afraid?

GREGORY: He is a young man yet,
      And yet is fearful for the wrath of gods!

JOACHIM: O Christ, what hope, while these thy ministers
      Threaten men's sin with beams wrenched from thy cross,
      And tyrannize o'er tyranny for thee?   395

CONSTANTINE: Lords, have we sounded peace about the land,
      Or won the borders of the realm from war,
      That we should find, before our very face,
      Strife, malice?

THEODORIC: To the king I make appeal.

INNOCENT: I also, who am called his Justicer.   400

THEODORIC: Is this the measure of thy justice? King,
It is the rule and custom of the land
That we, thy lords, have power on our own men
In our own woods; my man hath slain my beast.
I claim the slayer, by justice of the king. 405

CONSTANTINE: It is the purpose of our fathers, use
Of all our princes, each in his degree,
In his due bound due lordship to maintain.
We so uphold it.

THEODORIC: Let the king then charge
His Justicer to yield the man who flies 410
To yonder convent from his doom and me.

CONSTANTINE: Cousin, we think not the Lord Abbot stands
Antagonist of so strong heart against
Thy right, the land's law, above all our will.

INNOCENT: Is judgement given? may a monk yet speak? 415

CONSTANTINE: Speak: if, my lord, it is but to recall
Thy train and this man's vassal.

INNOCENT: (And may God
So call my soul back from salvation as
I deal with that man!) Hear, my lord the king!
This claim is on the base of ancient law 420
Against the Order and myself advanced.
Questionless must the Justicer uphold
All law; wherein offenses have due place:
Great wrongs call first for judgement, relegate
The lesser evil to the later time. 425
Since our accuser hath let pass this man,
And dared no whit against the shaven priests
His guard (moved by what peaceful thought or fear
We know not), we demand our greater claim
Be heard and first adjudged: what saith the king? 430

CONSTANTINE: Speak; only on full audience we decree.

INNOCENT: I accuse my lord Theodoric, who urged
His servants to a vile and outlaw deed;
Of grievous and malicious evil, wrought
Against the right of the clergy and the Church, 435
Against admitted right of sanctuary;
I accuse of breaking custom, law, and use
General with us, my lord Theodoric.
Shall I have justice?

CONSTANTINE: Much this is to claim.
What privilege we gave we yet uphold, 440
Nor lightly ever do resume our gift.
But—

A LORD: Must the king's word stool a chair of pride?

THEODORIC: God's death, what boldness, abbot,—

Another LORD: Hear me, king.—

INNOCENT: Nay, let me yet hold place for other words:
Ere which I here lay off and here resign 445
All office. Chancellor and Justicer
Am I no longer. From thy princes, king,
Thy chiefs, thy men of war, thy mountaineers,
Choose men in government and civil law
Learnèd, to order forth the realm. For me, 450
This thing was never got of olden time,
Not learned of peoples or of elders' mouths,
Not custom of dead lords, charter of kings,
But holy! And anathema are they
Who tear the thief, the manslayer, the forsworn, 455
From any these God's altars—how much more
If for a dead dog peace and sanctity
Of the Church yet violate, taking again
That which is corban and ascript to God,
Working a crowned honour out of thorn!— 460
Meet sons of proper fathers!

CONSTANTINE: Good my lord,
This is no such great matter, whe'er it be
That way or this determined, to whose gain—

INNOCENT: Wilt thou say which things shall seem great or small
In God's sight ever? King, art thou avised 465
By councillors, of what He maketh much
Or what He counteth naught? Nay then, enough!
Thou hast no need of priesthood more: Thy word
(Which how was armed we say not, nor inquire
Whether indeed it saved the realm from foes, 470
Or therein healed the pestilence) is strong.
To send one man of all these, and forbid
The building-up of yonder convent walls,
Repeal thy gifts of land, exile us all,
We without prayer will go forth. From their desks 475
The shaven clerks within thy chancery,
The upper clergy on thine embassies,
The priests, or leeches in the hospitals
Or masters in the schools, or overseers,
Surveyors of the land, sowers of crops, 480
And the religious from within their cells
Shall all pass forth:—I wait not for thy word,—

CONSTANTINE: Thou shalt not surely leave me, lest again
The malediction fall upon the land!

INNOCENT: Who is it shall deny our passage? King, 485
We are not to be cajoled thus and chid!
Thou art the Church's servant or her foe:
Choose.

CONSTANTINE: If we—

INNOCENT: Choose: God's or the devil's.

CONSTANTINE: Thine!

INNOCENT: Say'st thou? Let these thy lords declare their will.

[*The* LORDS *nearest the* KING *are silent: others in the outer circles speak.*]

The LORDS: Thou shalt not go.—Who else apportions land? 490
Didst thou not do me right?—Thou shalt not go;

The Chapel of the Thorn 61

	Because thou hast shown us beauty and fair life.—	
	Go not: the cities are thy friends, whose trade	
	Along new roadways pushes in thy guard.—	
	Peace hast thou brought and time for harvest. —Stay,	495
	For God's sake, also for our sakes, God's sons.	

INNOCENT: In all things shall our rights be kept?

CONSTANTINE: In all:
Only herein we pray thee give us leave
To hold our cousin scatheless: after this
Shall no heart beat nor mouth speak toward thy harm.   500

INNOCENT: Willingly we forget a moment's wrath.
Hereafter shall the man who fled be named
Among our vassals, and henceforth all strife—

THEODORIC: Church-vassal, ha?

INNOCENT: Church-vassal: lords there be
Who overtread the crops of lordless men   505
Smiting their huts and them with hate and fire,
Who will not bring torch near, nor thresholds cross
Despitefully where sandalled feet have trod.

CONSTANTINE: Enough, all strife is ended now; let be.
Yet none the less, lord Abbot, we had deemed   510
This Joachim was disobedient, held
Thy foe, and to be roughly governed.

INNOCENT: Sir,
The brain must teach and use the body, so.
The Church controls at will the secular arm,
Which hath, except thereby, no power to move.   515
Neither are all deeds that a king may do
Meet undertaking for his lords, but now,
If the king please, behold the Chapel here.

CONSTANTINE: Let the priest Joachim of Holy Thorn
Stand forth.

JOACHIM: I, king, am here.

CONSTANTINE: Make answer, then: 520
              Make thy defense before us.

JOACHIM: At whose charge
              Comes up the state of the land against my age?

CONSTANTINE: That thou art obstinate in thine own will
              Against the abbot delegated here
              By edict of the Apostolic See,   525
              Whom we profess desire and strength to serve,
              This were no small thing: thou hast sinned yet more,
              Teaching unheard-of doctrine, that God wills
              No man to be obedient or to hold
              Creeds learned of wise men set to teach the poor. 530
              Heresy and rebelling (which before
              We thank God that we knew not),—thou defiest
              Abbot and king.

JOACHIM: King-abbot, abbot-king!
              Aye: I have waited long until this hour.
              Thine is it ye should swear yourselves allies   535
              To work a masterdom on soul and flesh,—
              Against man's unity a unity.

INNOCENT: Have we no cause for that we do? Thy words
              Are more than common men may understand.

JOACHIM: None shall impeach thy deed of fault therein.   540

CONSTANTINE: Continually dost thou accuse our laws.

JOACHIM: Into what law wert thou baptized, O king?
              Or rather to what freedom?

CONSTANTINE: Aye, this talk
              Moves all the land to mutiny.

JOACHIM: What then?
              Are not these poor folk whom God died for, freed 545
              From any law except Christ's pulse in theirs,

	And irregularly his in each one beats.	
	But yet,—of old ye bound him, and again	
	Upon his body, would ye lock your chains.	
INNOCENT:	Because a man be poor and ill at ease,	550
	Upon the broad road shall he find out God?	
	With no large promises of freedom we	
	Exalt low hearts toward glad things: let them pay	
	Their due of righteous living first to God.	
JOACHIM:	How can their poor oppression pay such lives?	555
INNOCENT:	It is less matter if all thrones of kings	
	Be shaken into nothing than that one	
	Of all these least men should fall short and sin	
	In deed, in word, even in a little thought:	
	Which if they needs must do, or needs must break	560
	Out of their dungeons into spacious walks	
	Which all may hold in equal privilege,	
	The choice 'twixt such necessities be theirs:—	
	The Church unswerving holds upon her way.	
CONSTANTINE:	How then, lord abbot?	
INNOCENT:	Be contented, king.	565
	For needs must be, while men together dwell,	
	Civil constraint and formal government,	
	Whereof in necessary process lords	
	May in due rank compel and be compelled,	
	So they exceed no natural power of law,	570
	Which ere we exercise, consider well,	
	Brother; appointed priest, wilt thou not set	
	Example to these laymen, lords and carles,	
	Of righteousness and duty owed to God?	
JOACHIM:	What duty hath the void to that uprush	575
	Of wind which makes and fills it? or what debt	
	Is to the waters of the whirlpool due	
	From pillared hollows that themselves effect?	
	It is a word angels perchance may use,	
	Not men.	

INNOCENT:	We spend the time unduly. Yield:	580
	Or we by force tomorrow seize the Thorn.	

JOACHIM: Perchance there shall be war before I yield.

CONSTANTINE: War! My lord abbot?...

INNOCENT: War! thou—*thou* wilt war
Evil to conquer evil?

JOACHIM: I compel
The hearts of none; yet if, for their souls' sake, 585
Men gather about me crying freedom, God
Hath plucked up help for me and marshalled war.

INNOCENT
  [*to a MONK*]: Call yonder headman here.
  [*To the KING*]: It cannot be.
He dreams; the village fights not for the Thorn,
Who barely, as we heard, maintain the Faith. 590
There is more in it. Call the headman.
  [*He sees AMAEL*] Ha!
Earrings of gold and a sword! a harp-player!
Are the old evils loose again? Doth sin
Of darkness, blood, do gods of earth and sea
Lift head from that abyss Christ hurled them to. 595
  [*To the PRIOR*]:
Have yonder harp-player hither: see'st thou?
  [*To GREGORY*]: Aye,
Thou art the head-man?

GREGORY: Men have called me so.

INNOCENT: Speak, then: what war is this ye make on us?

CONSTANTINE [*apart to INNOCENT*]:
It must not be, lord abbot; all the land
Frets even yet, and is amazed at peace. 600
The flinging of one spear, although it strike
But on our shield, will after it draw on
Those discontents which still make sharp their blades.

INNOCENT:	Sir,—
CONSTANTINE:	Nay, consider!
INNOCENT [to GREGORY]:	

                        Son, when I return
Be at the convent: thou shalt take no harm,   605
Our word for't! what thou hast of grievance plead.
Be gone!

JOACHIM: Hold yet thy purpose in thy mind!
Cleave to the sacred knowledge of thy heart!

GREGORY: That whereof we, peasants, poor folk, are sure,
No priestly hand shall lightly strike away.   610

                                  [*He goes out.*

INNOCENT: Sir, yet by leave. Son John, who is this man?

JOHN: Who are thou, fellow?

AMAEL: I am a little dust
Blown from the ruined temples of the gods
And troubled by the feet of the white Christ
When he goes through the land.

JOHN: Art thou baptized?   615

AMAEL: Aye, with a baptism that ye know not of,
Who sit in lifelong dreams and silent prayers.
Have ye no need to be baptized of me,
That I should come to you to be baptized?

JOHN: Fellow,—

INNOCENT: Be silent. Say to me thy name.   620

AMAEL: I am a singer, a minstrel of the gods,
A priest in mine own office even as thou,
And have a name therein that none may speak
Who call me Amael in the light of the sun.

JOHN:	Thy gods were gods of that West-country king,	625
	The place of whose nation is a sepulchre,	
	And he himself gone to his gods in hell.	

AMAEL: With a king's swords ye overthrew a king,
But not with swords or boasting or carved wood
Shall ye destroy the gods, the Rider by Night, 630
The Singer of Strife, the Flame about the Wild!

CONSTANTINE: Surely this singer is an enemy,
A stray, a reckoner-up of lands, men, herds,
Strongholds; whereof to bear his master word.
He serves my foes,— let him be bound and slain! 635

INNOCENT: To please my lord, because he is a priest,
To let him be delivered to my hand
For death or exile or imprisoning!

CONSTANTINE: He is a spy, lord abbot, sent to learn
The highroads of our peace and husbandry! 640

INNOCENT: What foeman hath my lord the king to fear?

CONSTANTINE: Hath not this fellow's lord, whoe'er he be,
Planned evil on my heritage?

INNOCENT: Why then,
Let the king send his servant back with gold
Or jest of his discovery, whereto 645
If my lord will, let there be added threats,
Lest this same master should suppose we fear.

CONSTANTINE: There is no king or prince of any land
Whom we in any wise can fear. Be't so,
Lord abbot: speak to him and set him free. 650

INNOCENT: Fitting is such command to royal lips:
For freedom is the craftsmanship of kings,
Though somewhat they use pain therein for tool.

CONSTANTINE: In which kings' craft thy wisdom, my good lord
roves near as skilled a worker as ourselves. 655

INNOCENT:	Nay, while your Highness such obedient son	
	Shows still to the Church in doctrine and in deed,	
	In faith and morals born of faith, we joy	
	To hold ourselves in all things secular	
	The servant and the subject of the king.	660
CONSTANTINE:	And willingly we to thy zeal commit	
	These lighter matters: for ourselves are bound	
	Ere vespers to hold counsel on new schemes	
	To raise a new and necessary tax.	

[*The KING and his train move on.*]

INNOCENT [*to the PRIOR*]:
        Send these men hence: keep but the stranger here.   665
[*To the KING as he departs*]:
        Under which head consider, Sir, the pleas
        Advanced by the masters of the harbour late
        (The brethren of the Exchequer hold the notes):
        The harvest in the North is spoiled, all tax
        Must be remitted for a season: gold   670
        Hath been of late dug out—please it my lord
        To keep the council sitting till I come!

[*The MONKS disperse the people and follow them away. One speaks to INNOCENT as he returns in thought.*]

The MONK:	The master of the music sends to know	
	If the new chants shall be rehearsed to-night.	
INNOCENT:	The new chants... aye... in our Lady's chapel. Stay,	675
	Do the six voices serve?	
The MONK:	Yes, father.	
INNOCENT:	Good.	
	After the council bid him wait on us.	

[*The MONK goes out.
There remain MICHAEL,
JOACHIM, AMAEL,
INNOCENT, and JOHN.
It is drawing towards twilight.
INNOCENT comes slowly
down till he stands opposite to
AMAEL. They look steadfastly
one on the other, and
INNOCENT speaks.*

INNOCENT: I am a monk, a servant of my God,
A priest in mine own office, even as thou:
And little like to think of death therein,   680
By the grace of God His Mother, even as thou:
For, knowing there is naught here to be gained,
What hast thou in thy heart? behold, for naught,
Much hast thou dared.

AMAEL: But thou hast dared yet more.
For I, if ye should slay me, take away   685
In this my venture mine own life, but thou
Wouldst take away the lives of many men
In making a great silence of our songs.

INNOCENT: But we have given men other songs to sing.
Chants that may be as watchwords in their fight,   690
Their outpost strife in that deific war
Which threats the sleeping village of the world.

AMAEL: O pleasant to the hearing of a priest!

INNOCENT: Shall a priest's voice make mockery of a priest,
Who hath not taught thy kindred to mock thee?   695

AMAEL: Thou would have taught them worse things, had they learned.

INNOCENT: Enmity.

AMAEL: O the white cheeks of your Christ.
They can be red with anger then? His mouth
Perchance is dumb with fury, not with fear?

INNOCENT:	Ye have already wrought out upon God	700
	All that the devils of your altars bade!	
	How should He fear now, though He then had feared?	
	His anger is not vengéd upon men,	
	Nor slays He any foes for slaying's sake…	
	Which on what altars hath what priesthood done?	705
AMAEL:	Twice hath my hand lain over mortal eyes,	
	While, with the incantation of the Fire,	
	I struck forth human blood upon the stone!	
INNOCENT:	O slayer of Christ!	
AMAEL:	O Christ's serf, take and slay!	
INNOCENT:	I have power to slay, and to release have power.	710
AMAEL:	Slay, then. I die, but the strong gods remain.	
	Thou canst not dig so deep a well, nor build	
	Chapels of such walled thickness, that therein	
	Earth and the dawn-star shall not shake man's heart.	
	Abbot, though but one man were left, one saint,	715
	Sworn, shaven, bent to watching, in one room,	
	One little lonely chamber hewn in rock,	
	While he moved lips, or even spread in prayer	
	Hands Christward, there should thirst and hunger be,	
	Love and hate, eating and drinking, wrath and fear.	720
	There should the gods have prayer and service; yea,	
	Though all men perish,—if wild beasts remain,	
	Seeking at night about the woods for prey,	
	Them the gods rend with hunger, and abide.	
JOACHIM:	Brother, thy gods are diverse: God is one.	725
	Yet herein hast thou seen and spoken well,	
	That where one beast, one stone is, God is there.	
	His will and man's will are; and what more powers	
	He hath created to free use of will	
	Have therein separate being; save for this,	730
	There is naught of matter or spirit but is God,	
	Yea all man's being, save his will, is God.	

AMAEL:	Long shall no will prevail against my gods.
	Hunger and thirst of every sort, a fire
	Lit in the lustihood of flesh shall burn 735
	All but the very fire itself,—the law,
	The Thorn, the Cross, the name of Christ: albeit
	For a little while can ye make men afraid.

JOACHIM: Let rather men be bold to sin than be
O'erruled by terror. Naught is any worth   740
If ye destroy a man's heart in his breast,
Or change to fear his valiancy of soul.

INNOCENT: Here is consent of counsel! Against me
Are ye come up, O brethren newly sworn?
Lo, thine ally in freedom, Joachim!   745
For who shall sever in the common ear,
Yea, even to wise hearts who shall well divide
The end of this man's way from thine? Sir priest,
Doth any power at all compel the gods?

AMAEL: Ye are wise men and know the mighty gods   750
Are called immortal, over us: their lives
Sufficient are to them; in youth or eld
As first they broke to being, so they are.
They drive man's generations as a wind
Tosses in wave on wave to shoreward: time   755
Dwells not amid their might, for centuries
Pass at their feasts in one cup-lifting. Yet
There is a darkness beyond all the gods,
Where once in many ages that which Is
In Its eternal sleep whose dreams we are   760
Heaves suddenly and shudders half-awake.
Then, as an earthquake rends the seas and shores
Making all strange, so the All-being moves,
And all the visible and invisible worlds
In that sole motion ruin and are re-born   765
Into fresh lands, new nations, other gods.

INNOCENT: And therefore did I well to drive you all,
Bards of the ancient legends, from the land.
And therefore now I drive thee forth again.

	O fool, care we at all for names of gods,	770
	Heroes, kings, warriors, stories told by night?	
	If this were all, ye should come up and sing	
	In mine own parlour before vespers! No,	
	But now ye bards who more than common wise	
	Profess yourselves in sight of things to be	775
	Have this alone to teach when all is taught,	
	That choice is none for us 'twixt heaven or hell,	
	'Twixt evil and good, because such heaven and hell	
	Such purpose, hope, despair, content, and joy	
	Are naught beneath the gods, and they are naught	780
	Beneath the Darkness whence all things were born,	
	In Nothing's dream of being:—which shall ye teach?	
	See to it; in three days' time get thee hence	
	Lest worse things smite on thee! in three days! Go.	

AMAEL: Fear not; I go, who was a little wroth 785
Because I heard no voice from any hut
When I sent one last song about the hills…
Yet would I run before thee through the land
And at some secret pool, ere it reflect
The fingers of thy benediction, fill 790
One brimming cup which when I come to die,
I may in sacrifice pour out on earth,
Saying, *With this water which no Christ hath blessed*
Do I, their priest, salute the immortal gods.

[*He goes out. After a moment*
MICHAEL slips away to
follow him.

INNOCENT: The dragon that would rend the earth hath lashed 795
The poisonous meres of hell into a storm,
Whereof some spray is beaten against the world.
Which, lest in any wise we should forbid
Drink to one soul in the dessert of his life,
We, being fearful, do of late neglect. 800

[*He looks out after AMAEL;*
and turns then to JOACHIM.

How long, my brother?

JOACHIM: Even until I die.

INNOCENT: Nay, let thy hands yield now what they shall loose
            At the death-hour. What fixed pride is this?
            Hopeless and purposeless of any end,
            What seekest thou to gain?

JOACHIM: It is enough   805
            If ye and yours gain nothing till I die:
            When it may be that Michael my son
            Shall be a voyager for God's sake, as
            For God's sake I a sojourner have been.

INNOCENT: Think it not so. To-morrow or to-day   810
            Thy son or thou shalt give and we shall take
            (Though thou and I be dead) the blessed Thorn.

JOACHIM: Little then shall it profit thee, being dead:
            The which is no small matter, for indeed
            What more hast thou at heart than only this,   815
            Means of advancement to high place, and power
            Over the heart and conscience of the king?

JOHN: Out, slanderous mouth! out, grey-haired liar!

INNOCENT: Peace.
            Say'st thou? What more?

JOACHIM: In hunger for much land
            And greediness of rule, through these twelve years,   820
            Hast thou lift up thy head above the king
            To make men fear thy tumult of big words.
            'Hell', say'st thou, 'the eternal worm', 'the fire',
            'God', say'st thou, and 'salvation' say'st thou.
            'The keys of heaven and hell' thou sayest; so.   825
            Keys of the royal treasury hast gained.
            'Sword of Saint Paul' thou sayest, and therewith
            Above all lords hast word in peace or war.
            O merchant of the mysteries! …Only here
            Thou hast not yet found profitable trade.   830

INNOCENT:	Let then my voice meet here with equal voice.	
	Now, lest I think thy heart hath only hope	
	Of larger offer and more liberal grant,	
	Set out thine accusation. Stand and speak.	
	What say'st of Innocent, thou, Joachim?	835
JOACHIM:	That thou hast found in traffic through the world	
	The riches of Christ's blood are vendible,	
	And therewithal hast bought to thine own use	
	The might and splendours of a temporal rule.	
	Thou hast made laws for men: thou wilt bow down	840
	With fear of prison each man's thoughts and lusts,	
	To a baptism into Faith and Love.	
	Which dare ye call salvation? O false tongue	
	For not until the life of any man,—	
	Whereof his heart hath heard the rustling leaves,	845
	But knows not beyond what shut door it grows,—	
	Is drenched with rains of mercy,—then the hand	
	Of the Gardener thereof undoes the gate,	
	And he goes in and labours thereabout	
	Till from a sapling a great tree be grown,	850
	And all his days eat blessed fruit thereof,—	
	Not until then shall any law be worth	
	Nor shall the service of his will be sure.	
	But thou hast sworn him to a lawyer's code,	
	Religion hast thou made a fair for kings	855
	And bred the soul of man to market-drudge.	
INNOCENT:	And keeps she not her house within the world?…	
	Stern is thy heart toward us and harsh thy voice	
	With an accusing word of land and gold.	
	Perchance there be among us bribed of earth;	860
	And true it is the Church hath fashioned forth	
	A creed for thought and word, a law for act,	
	To make obedient (so to keep secure)	
	Her children. Wilt thou that each man should form	
	To his own hope and for his own control,	865
	Out of his dim and momentary days,	
	An aim, or creed, a doctrine, and a law?	
	Must each man learn the dialects of God	
	Not as a child learns, being taught, but as	
	The whole world stumbled slowly into speech?	870

JOACHIM:	Is not each man a new world before God,
	With his own winds, earthquakes, and nights? alone,
	As any incommunicable star?

INNOCENT:	Which in the will and strength of God the Law,	
	Or fixed, or moved in planetary spheres,	875
	Toward others hath control and is controlled!	

JOACHIM: Ah, maintenance of things, which never man
Shall find, except through his own strength of love.

INNOCENT: Nay, by law only shall men find out love,
The greater from the lesser: being loosed,   880
He should seek after love in anarchy.
But what love is that is not in itself
Absolute law? which law, made visible,
Audible in the advent of God's self
(Whereof we are the echo through the years)   885
Is the direction and control of man.
Who, bound upon a journey, comes by night
To an abyss, and, treading the one plank,
The single bridge of his own life, feels out
With either hand for succour, till he clasp   890
That which hath been, and is to be, and is,
Doctrine and bar of dogma, at his side.
Else, blown upon by winds of breath and thought,
And doubting whether any voice indeed
Called from the opposite darkness, his heart fail,   895
His feet slip, and he go down quick to hell.

JOACHIM: Say rather, if a stranger come by night
To a king's house, and enter in the porch,
Where, finding some small shelter from the wind,
He sit, saying 'Lo, at length am I come home',   900
The whilst within his king hath poured the wine,—
So thy disciples are content! Alas,
How few of all those many who through years
Obey thy government and speak thy creed
Shall with how little wisdom understand   905
That purpose! even how few among thy priests
Shall know wherein they minister and rule!
Lo, thy successor at thy hand!—Prior John,
Once more, what charge is this thou layest on me?

The Chapel of the Thorn

INNOCENT:	Nay, but… Speak then, my son!	910

JOHN: What else but that which, reverend father, thou
Hast waged against this disobedient soul
How often! that himself will not obey,
But with strange talk makes stubborn all this folk?
Against thy will and name who art come down, 915
Armed with the king's swords and decrees from Rome
To hold above the faithful judicature?

JOACHIM: And to what end hath he that judicature?

JOHN: To rule the faithful and expound the Faith.

JOACHIM: Wherefore should he hold rule on other men? 920

JOHN: To gain a better ordering through the Church.

JOACHIM: Speak it not, speak it not! for thou hast ta'en
A word upon thy lips that is not thine.
Thy Church is but in censers, altar-lights,
Coming and going from confessionals:— 925
How should I yield the Thorn up to such thought?
Who have beheld the holy Bride, the Church,
Caught to her mystic marriage through the world,
Wed to her Lover in all mortal things;
Spirit, which is the will of man, being knit 930
To bodily form, which is the will of God.
Therefore her going is like sound of springs,
Clasp of her hand is as the strength of bread,
Her voice shall make men drunken as with wine.
Her sorrow is the travail of all earth. 935
In all things' aspiration she aspires;
In the desire of beasts unhungered, in
The falling star, the lightning of the storm,
And in the beating of birds' wings abroad,
She hungers and she lightens and she throbs. 940
Yet still articulate in human speech,
And visible in spread of mortal hands,—
This is the spiritual verity,
This is the Church, this is salvation, this!
And will ye make it sure to men by law? 945

INNOCENT:	Blessed thy soul is that hath seen these things,	
	Blessed thy mouth that speak them. Yet, not less,	
	I too have borne much penance, fasted long,	
	(I speak as a fool,) seen visions, and dreamed dreams.	
	I would make sure the highways till God's feet	950
	Go safely up and down throughout the world.	
	Securely shall He go! securely man	
	Shall freely move to his predestined end.	
	And how should these things be, except by law?	
	For man's soul is but as a little child	955
	God caught up to His arms on Calvary;	
	Whence with His horsemen through His foes he drives	
	One world-rush to His city: in whose hands	
	Are maces of iron dogma, beating down	
	The crests and shields of false philosophies.	960
	Lonely and far ye ride, O saints! but we	
	Rally and charge about the soul of man.	
	Go, Joachim, wake the adulterer from sleep	
	Or on the knife-hilt stay the murderous hand,	
	Not once or twice, but times on thousand times,	965
	Till this world's axis wholly hath been changed!	
	Ah, brother, few among this place have left,	
	For all thy teaching of elect desire,	
	Their lemans, yet in half a hundred weeks,	
	Before Saint Cyprian twice hath seen the sun,	970
	I will break up this custom, wherein men	
	Wander astray and lose themselves from light.	
JOACHIM:	Aye, thou by proclamation or decree,	
	On penalty of forfeiture of land,	
	Or fine of labour, in the end perchance	975
	Death, wilt by force forbid concubinage.	
	By law a man must love his wife,—and shall!	
INNOCENT:	There shall be neither forfeit, fine, nor death	
	At our desire; spiritual the sin,	
	Spiritual the penalty shall be:	980
	The man be excommunicate, outlaw	
	From mass, and from all holy things, and from	
	Place in our courts ecclesiastical…	
	What wilt thou? wilt thou teach these village-men	
	The mystery of this, Love's sacrament,	985

	Yet, till their lives have learned that First and Last,	
	Alpha and Omega of God's ways with men,	
	Deny to them the single certain way	
	Of learning such dear wisdom, in the life	
	That treads, though hardly, with shut eyes, the Law?	990

JOACHIM: Save a man's will be gained, his life is naught.

INNOCENT: Nay, by life only shall a man's will learn.—
In which cause therefore I demand again,
Wilt thou yield up to me this Crown of Thorn,
And join thy will to our own will, and make   995
One creed, one law for all this people?

JOACHIM: No.
Thou hast mine answer; do thy will.

                                            [*He goes up to the Chapel.*

INNOCENT: Son John,
Knowest thou there goes a greater man than we?

JOHN: Rebel he is, …and heretic perchance,…
He, greater?

INNOCENT: Yet when, coming from the Mount,   1000
The face of Moses shone, his guiding then
Had dazzled all the people to their woe.

JOHN: He takes too much upon him: he is one
Who will not bow his stiff neck down to men,
To thee, my father, nor to me, nor Rome.   1005
Hold him not easily, bring him to trial,
Seeing rebellion is so dire a sin.

INNOCENT: Never two men stood up with hungry hearts
And against power in the name of God
Made bare the sword, but God was there a third.   1010

JOHN: Is he not shown forth in authority?

INNOCENT: Aye, in authority and in revolt,
The parting and the gathering.—Joachim
Hath seen, and follows that he saw till death.
He with all saints may climb high paths, and tread   1015
O'er spiritual precipices, breathe
The chill air of supernal Thought: but we,
Who hold the monstrance of the common heart,
The bad unrestful heart of common men,
In lifted hands, processional toward God,   1020
With care-toiled watch set foot in front of foot
Along the slow steep sureness of the Way;
Diverse to each diversity must prove,
Voice to the blind and vision to the deaf,
Time for the lame man, of the dumb man speech,—   1025
Which how should saints, rapt to their mystery, be?
Therefore the greater shall be overthrown
And the lesser man shall conquer, …even I.
Come.

                              [*They go out.*

Act II

[*MICHAEL is sitting on the cliff, looking seaward. AMAEL and a VILLAGER come up from the lower shore.*

The VILLAGER:	They hear all speech among us, and at least
	Will venge Themselves on who hath scouted Them.
AMAEL:	But then shall all who fought for them be rich
	With silver, oxen, and comely maid.
The VILLAGER:	Aye, that were well indeed if one might guess 5
	Who of Them should have store of gifts at last.
	But this none know, nor who shall win, nor if
	Some yet unknown lord shall not overcome.
	Therefore I hold it wise (for there is use
	Of witchcraft in the Thorn and thee, each way 10
	Is peril in Their malice toward my harm)
	To walk with heed of danger that we know;
	As, not to journey under a new moon,
	Nor speak by tombs of aught that we hold dear,
	And always else to keep shut lips, until 15
	They 'twixt Themselves agree, for I have seen
	Ill chances fall to them that talked of gods.

[*He goes on his way.*

AMAEL:	O Fire of the Wild, come swiftly and burn up
	These fearful men;—whom thou, white Christ, perchance
	Befriendest, since thine own disciples fled! 20

[*He goes up to MICHAEL.*

	How long before the next strange vessel pass?
MICHAEL:	Whither lies land the nearest?
AMAEL:	There, and there.
MICHAEL:	And thither go thy vessels?

The Chapel of the Thorn

AMAEL:	South thereof.

AMAEL: South thereof.
Because the Southern towns most glad the sight
Of the sea-riders, and the Southern lands   25
For wage or ransom are of all most rich.

MICHAEL: Whom will ye put to ransom?

AMAEL: Cities, kings:
Three sea-ports have I seen to Gorlias
Send their best wealth for purchase of their lives,
One hundred golden chains; of silver bars   30
As many thrice; then shirts of ringèd mail;
Of swords, spears, axes, weapons of offense,
As many as outweighed the silver bars;
Three boys—the best of all their slaves—to be
Pages to Gorlias; one to bear my harp;   35
And wine and meat till after seven days
The wind blew seaward and we sailed away.
That is good stuff for song!

MICHAEL: What song was that
Thou sang'st before the moon rose yesternight
While down the way beneath went by the crowd   40
Of men and women toward the lower shore?

AMAEL: The song of the wooing and marriage of Oedh the king,
And how he wrought enchantment for his bride.

MICHAEL: And after that?

AMAEL: I sang thee many songs.
Which of them all hath waked thee, flesh and soul?   45

MICHAEL: Last night I dreamed that on this cliff I saw
How the lord abbot strove with Joachim,
Till the earth split beneath them, and they twain
Slipped into darkness, and the Chapel fell.
Then there came forth wild riders from the sea,   50
Clouded, with lightnings in their hands, a noise
About them as if ancient forests burned,
And howl of wolves.

AMAEL: Ha, hast thou seen the gods?

MICHAEL: But when their horses' hooves struck land they too
Were swallowed in earth's opening. Then the sea 55
Burst into that abysm after them,
And broke the cliff down whereupon I stood;
So that I fell, through neither sea nor land,
But chaos, till a great wave caught me up
And hurled me to a boat, wherein there sailed 60
After their nightly labour fishermen
Of the village with their meagre spoil toward home.
What should this mean?

AMAEL: They are! …they are not! …Boy,
Wert thou not Arcus' son?

MICHAEL: Aye.

AMAEL: Then wert thou
Born of a giant, a wrestler, good at arms, 65
The biggest man of all this shore, who yet,
Being heart-careless of the world and fame,
Flung in the sea his meshéd years of life,
As a fisher's net, to draw a little haul
Of common deeds,—as thou wilt do, his son. 70

MICHAEL: The headman and the priest have no thought else.—
What else?

AMAEL: Yet one who was high-priest ere I
Would fain have chosen him for harp-bearer
To voyage with himself and a king's son
(The elder brother of King Constantine): 75
But, whether idleness or lack of care
For unknown things held him, he would not go.
Therefore I took the harp and in his stead
Learned song and journeying and sorcery,—
As thou, his son, might'st learn of me.

MICHAEL: I, learn! 80
Wouldst thou…?

AMAEL: We boarded an Italian ship,
And won much gold, but little glory; thence,
Eastward and inland,—gods!—till I beheld
A storm of arméd men beat down on earth
And knew that underneath the cloud was Rome. 85

MICHAEL: Before my lord the Abbot came, old wives
Would vow to children this or that should be
When Rome falls: and I know that month by month
Thither he sends, and hears, and sends again.
What is this Rome to be a name with men? 90

AMAEL: Boy, thou hast questioned all man's heart in this;
For through what might can one small city's name
Outdo her arms in power on utmost shores
Till the extreme lands round about the world
Seem but the lower slopes of seven mounts 95
Upon whose pleasant inner side is Rome?
And wherefore do their rulers, chiefs of tribes
Whose sires were bears and sea-lions, and they gods,
In Roman offices claim Roman names,
Praetor or consul, or desire to hold 100
Their lordship from the Roman Pope in fee?
So, while the near barbarians throng on her
Kings of more barbarous lands obey: her voice
Across wild foes calls upon wilder friends:
The godless dread her and the high gods fear. 105
With light is her enduring buttresséd,
And her foundation out of darkness hewn,
And nothing mortal can have power on her,
Till at the last the ancient blindworm Time,
Thrusting through Earth and burrowing, makes loose 110
The pedestal of her infrangible name
Which then shall like a pillar 'neath the worlds
Crash, and from dreams awaken That which Is.

MICHAEL: But wilt thou teach me?

AMAEL: Yet, until this be,
We will not lose nor cast down nor forget 115
One shrine that thou hast conquered, O great Rome!

MICHAEL: But wilt thou choose me for thy harp-bearer?

AMAEL: Art thou not sworn to Mary and the Christ?

MICHAEL: Shall Joachim prevent, if I would go?
Or shall I be compelled to service here 120
Till I like him grow old in years and learn
Christ's meaning?—if it may be learnt at all!

AMAEL: In far lands we shall die, …though we die kings!

MICHAEL: I would be slain in a great fight: but where,
What matter?

AMAEL: Well said, warrior! Come then, 125
Thou hast well chosen! Is it time in youth
To wait upon white altars? Hark, the gods
Sing at their feasting, not as hermits sing!
We servants of the gods have heard their song,
And some of us are mad with their delight, 130
And some are lords of ships and raids and fire,
And some have crept into the black bear's den
With a torch and a spear and slain him; but we all
Are heroes, princes, champions! Come, for now
The lord of a king's household waits for me, 135
Ere he push forth his galleys! Were thine arms
Meant to yearn always toward the Christ in prayer
Or the pale goddess Mary of Sorrows? No,
Forget them, swear obedience to my gods
Who shatter with their hammers earth and sea, 140
And work for whom they love a throne of gold,
And the body of his foe without the door,
And a most beautiful woman at his will
Whose arms may be a footstool for his ears,
Who shall unloose his sandals and bring wine! 145

MICHAEL: I am theirs! I am thine! But thou wilt teach me song,
Sword-play, and ship-craft? I shall look on Rome?

AMAEL: Thou shalt see Rome and hew Rome and beyond!

[*The First VILLAGER, the WOMAN whose son was ill and a HILLMAN come in by the hill-path.*]

The WOMAN: In the mid-night his fever passed, whereat
He mended swiftly, and this morn hath ease. 150

The First VILLAGER: Well; …But have care lest yet perchance he fail:
My grandsire died of such a sickness.

The WOMAN: Nay,
Christ's Mother heard my prayer and made him whole.
I go to bear him to my hut,
Then come to thank her.

The First VILLAGER: Well, …'tis strange…

[*She goes out.*

Always 155
Prayer and thanksgiving house in women's mouths.

The HILLMAN: That is a true word: we amid the hills
Know that the gods help little, yet our wives
Still pray to them when keen eyes will suffice
And praise where sure feet only have been friends. 160

[*GREGORY and the Second and Third VILLAGERS come in.*

GREGORY: Then if he send to hear of our intent
What say ye?

The Third VILLAGER: They are many, though the king,
Having now peace, be loth to wake new war
Through lands but hardly quiet; we are few:
Therefore I would that for this old man's sake 165
We risk no evil to our lives; to us
What profit if the Thorn be here or there?

The Second VILLAGER: What chanced between you yesterday?

GREGORY: Much talk
Of fishing, and the tides, the nets, the folk:
And so of common customs and old ways,   170
And what men think or hope of Joachim.

The First VILLAGER: Learned he from thee what 'neath yon altar lies?

GREGORY: Nay, he is foolish who speaks forth to lords.
I told him naught he guessed not long before:
As, that of old this was a common place   175
For meetings 'twixt our towns of peace or war.
And therefore many tales of heroes grew
Ebbing and surging on it through the land,
As the sea on its base; nor Druhild least
(For fear by chance he should have heard that name).   180

The First VILLAGER: What promise made he?

GREGORY: That this place should still
Be open to us village men, a priest
Being from the convent sent here to sing mass
And be a watchman by it; that no law
Should exile tales of Druhild with the bards.   185

The First VILLAGER: Surely it is enough: our eyes shall see
When Druhild breaks the altar with one arm:
And reaches forth his other toward a beam.
Nor shall himself be hemmed in by a wall
Nor lost amid our children's ignorance   190
When he comes back to lead them.

The HILLMAN: Aye, enough:
If we may come down from the hills and stand
Around the door-posts to behold his tomb.

The Second VILLAGER: Is there none other custom worthy fight,
Though we use Druhild's name for war-cry?

The Third VILLAGER: None.   195

GREGORY: What wouldst thou?

The Third VILLAGER: Will not the lord abbot swear
(If he is grown so fain to have the Thorn
And fail the old man Joachim) to leave
All purchase of our women in our midst
As it hath been of old?

GREGORY: I know not that. 200
Hast thou not heard when Bros the hunter begged
Help of my lord, and justice on the man
Who stole his woman from him, when 'twas known
That he bought women other than his wife
My lord would hear him not, but drove him out 205
With anger?

The Second VILLAGER: Look, an hour is with us, such
As shall not soon again be: let us take
All that we can.

GREGORY: I am too old to fight
For pleasuring the pricking hands of youth.
Young men shall buy no maidens with my blood. 210

AMAEL [*breaking in upon their talk*]:
Old with more knowledge than should fight for girls,
Young with more ignorance than sees the gods,
Why wouldst thou fight, O Gregory?

GREGORY: For men
Whose speech is what our fathers knew, for time
That lasts when young men's sharp joys are forgot. 215
Love and the tales of God are naught to me,
But good is knowledge learned in stress of years.

The HILLMAN: Nay, we of the hills would fight for Druhild's tomb,
Because he was of us, but not to keep
Your wives and lemans in your fellowship 220

                Idly. If, as the headman tells, my lord
                Swear, then let be all strife.

The Third VILLAGER: Let be.

The First VILLAGER: Let be.

The Second VILLAGER: And yet methinks—

GREGORY: In good time! lo, my lord.

                [*INNOCENT comes in.*

INNOCENT: Benedicite, my sons: what answer?

GREGORY: Peace;
          If my lord wills to hold his promise sure   225
          Not to build walls about this place, nor hush
          The tales men tell of Druhild through the land.

INNOCENT: We promised so, and so will we perform:
          If on your part ye have no reason else
          To war against us or to hold the Thorn.   230

The Second VILLAGER [*half-aloud*]:
          A little promise… We withdrew much.

INNOCENT: Son,
What wouldst thou more?

The Third VILLAGER: Nay, he will ever talk.
          Heed him not, lord!

The Second VILLAGER: I have heard old Joachim
          Teach that man has but to find out God,
          And therefore was life given him?

INNOCENT: Aye; well?.   235

The Second VILLAGER: And that by love and the desire of man
　　　　　　　　　　Toward woman, may he learn thereof?

INNOCENT: 　　　　　　　　　　　　　　　　Aye; well?.

The Second VILLAGER: Which… if it be… my lord knows how of old
　　　　　　　　　　There was a custom… which lasts still, indeed,…
　　　　　　　　　　That there should be among us women changed…　　　　240
　　　　　　　　　　Bought… other than our wives…

INNOCENT: 　　　　　　　　　　　　　　　It may not be.
　　　　　　'I am a sword' God said, and swordlike now
　　　　　　The word of the Church divides the good and ill.
　　　　　　This is an ill thing.

The Second VILLAGER: 　　　　　　　　　Joachim then lied,
　　　　　　　　　　Teaching that God was in our midst and all　　　　　245
　　　　　　　　　　Desire was from him and toward him at last?

INNOCENT: Son, thou hast heard amiss.

The Second VILLAGER: 　　　　　　　　　　　　Mayhap. I heard
　　　　　　　　　　Joachim teach that only a man's will
　　　　　　　　　　Must be the rule and measure of his deed,
　　　　　　　　　　That by his doing what he would to the height　　　　250
　　　　　　　　　　Should he find out the… God.

INNOCENT: 　　　　　　　　　　　　　　And if he taught
　　　　　　That thou shouldst only work thy wicked will
　　　　　　He taught a damnable heresy, as thou
　　　　　　May'st find, in hell.

The Second VILLAGER: 　　　　　　Lord, I would work no harm!

INNOCENT: Thou lustest after women? And thy lord,　　　　　　　　　255
　　　　　Theodoric, would slay men at his will,
　　　　　And the king grind the poor to gain more gold,
　　　　　All so to live their lives out and find God!
　　　　　For now no crow or sparrow but must be
　　　　　Held noble as John's eagle; every cock　　　　　　　　　　260
　　　　　Struts on his dunghill like a mountain peak,

	And thinks himself as high above the flat,	
	Above the dusty ground of common law! …	
	O Joachim, my brother Joachim! …	
	As for ye, sirs of the village, get ye hence;	265
	Tread ye the law until ye find the love!	

                    [*The three* VILLAGERS *slip away.*

AMAEL: Yet wilt thou leave old stories in their mouths?
                Are not they also danger, abbot? When
                Shall thought of Druhild, called the Slayer of Kings,
                Seek grace from thought of Christ whom such kings slew?   270

INNOCENT: Thou that hast not begun to learn of Christ,
                Canst thou tell what tales hide within that word?
                Or how or when we priests, his vagrant bards,
                To slaves, to freemen, or to kings should teach
                His name; wherein all thoughts of Druhild move,   275
                Because it is the folklore of the world?

AMAEL: Nay; I was old in that ere he was born.
                I know the forest-paths, I know the caves
                Whence the first men crawled, with lean hands that clawed
                Like the wild beasts they learned their hunting from!   280
                I know the smell of blood upon the track
                Where first men snarled above the prey 'lo, mine!'
                I know the wantonness in women's eyes,
                The lust of cruelty in their masters' hands,
                And all the treacheries of the warring worlds!   285
                I have gone down and in a dark night laid
                My hands upon the leash of that desire
                Which evermore the gods let loose on us,
                And felt about my brows the wind-like lust
                That blows to changing shapes this mist of men!   290

INNOCENT: Thou hast gone near the making of the world.
                Yet of that old forgotten legendry,
                Those whispers of the flesh and soul, those lusts
                In passages of blood or thought, those dreams,
                Those hauntings of our fathers in ourselves,   295

	No voice, save of the Church, hath will to choose,	
	Knowledge to safeguard, strength to overthrow.	
	No voice but hers alone decrees aright:	
	'This is a rumour of religion; that,	
	A slander breathed by Satan out of hell.'	300
	So wise she is, so pitiful, so stern,	
	Because the Faith is older than all men.	
GREGORY:	Yet none among our fathers knew thy Faith.	
INNOCENT:	All men have known it as some ancient thing	
	That chanced to them or mayhap to their sires.	305
	And had thine own no tales for drinking time?	
GREGORY:	Stories of heroes and of kings at war.	
INNOCENT:	And therein was a torch lit, though it threw	
	But red light, dim with smoke and blown with wind,	
	Where the wise pagans lit their vestal lamps,	310
	Wherewith the candles on our altars burn,	
	At fire upon all household hearths, the light	
	That lights all men who come into the world,	
	The Christ, that was born man before man was.	
AMAEL:	Thou ravest. Shall one alien or one dead	315
	Be by a faith he hath not known redeemed?	
INNOCENT:	No man hath lived who hath not known the Faith.	
	For 'mid white snows or discovered seas,	
	In heathen realms beyond the East, whereto	
	Dare none but apostolic pathways lead,	320
	Or toward the mouth of hell that bounds the West,	
	And back as far as to the earliest fires	
	And circling round the foot of Judgement Hill,	
	In little streams of legend, pools of prayer,	
	Drunk from at sacred wells, or watering trees	325
	Held holy by unreasoning multitudes,	
	Flow the four rivers of Eden, that great stone	
	Therewith men sealed them up into Christ's tomb	
	Being by his resurrection rolled away.	
	Therefore there never was nor ever shall	330

	Be meeting under any moon or sun	
	For a god's worship or a hero's tale,
	But therein higher hymn and history
	Surge and become tumultuous in that flood
	Of waters loosened from the inland hills.	335

AMAEL: What matter then if thou should teach or I,
Because all teachings are of equal worth?

INNOCENT: Who hath supposed them so? What mind hath trod
To equal profit either thought of twain?
Or what blurred eyes have held the reedman's hut,   340
Poor and alone in robber-haunted fens,
More meet for all men's dwelling than that town
Which now is built and building, where through gates
Beaten and fashioned, through cause and consequence,
Up to the aerial certitudes of thought   345
Squares of broad virtues are, wind-swept by grace,
And streets made wide in vows and marriage-loves
'Neath pediments of temples virginal,
And conduits running Eden-streams, but wine
On city-feasts, and each way going up   350
To the open space of the Forum, where all hearts
Are citizen to the consular-heart of God,
Where justice is—of just men's brotherhood,
Freedom, and safety of all conscious things,
Closed in these white republican walls of Rome...   355
Whereto, O God, a little let me toil!

[*He goes out.*

AMAEL: What power makes this man dream as if he saw?

GREGORY: His talk is ever thus; of houses, towns,
Roads, bridges, waterways, knowers of tongues.
Eager he is that men should do, and apt   360
To mark their doing. I have heard him say,
Preaching before the king upon a feast,
That, since God acts not many times but once
For ever, when he—thou hast heard their tale—
Worked wood in Nazareth, to those who saw   365

	Dust fashioned he to stars and clay to men,	
	Wherein all those who labour have their part:	
	This I remember for that afterwards	
	Old Andreas the carpenter, who died,	
	Laughed at his toil, swearing he made the worlds.	370

AMAEL: Nor lied he, if thine Abbot did not lie…
Wilt thou have all men in thy city, monk?
There shall be yet some few who ride without.

> [*He goes up again to join
> MICHAEL.*

The HILLMAN: There shall be then no strife to-day?

GREGORY: No strife.

> [*The HILLMAN goes out.
> JOACHIM comes down from
> the Chapel.*

JOACHIM: There comes no further summons. By this hour   375
From the new convent's castellated gates
Issues the train of bedesmen and of spears.
Brother, if still the village men uphold
Their freedom, will it please them I come down,
Or will they gather by the Chapel door?   380

GREGORY: I doubt they will not fight with any zeal.

JOACHIM: How! know they not what tyranny they face?
Know they not that this moment burns through time,
God in his great aspect when all good things
Shake on the verge of ruin, and Himself   385
Hardly—yet wholly—wins with them through war?
So once through Chaos, so on Calvary,
So still, a flame within their inmost hearts,
Against new usurpation of His rule?

GREGORY: Few men shall hold a danger to their souls   390
Worth peril of their bodies to prevent.

JOACHIM:	But know they not how small thing all else is?	
GREGORY:	Small! it is that we know we have,—a hut,	
	Talk with our kinsmen, wife or chamber-maid	
	To keep the hut, a sleeping-place, and food.	395
	Small! it is that we have.	
JOACHIM:	And they are ways	
	Whereby the soul aspires to God, whom won,	
	Except for His sake they are no more worth	
	Than candles burned out in solemnities	
	Which Innocent the Abbot makes for God.	400
	All doing is but littleness to them	
	Who, even as we, are, of His favour, ware,	
	By intellectual vision, mental sight,	
	Of that One primal and eternal Act,	
	Immanent and transcendent, wherein shine,	405
	Co-equal, co-eternal, consummate,	
	All purpose and all process and all end! …	
	Whereof is contemplation our best deed.	
GREGORY:	Talk, …talk: I know now: thou and the Abbot teach	
	This thing and that of the gods' deeds and ours.	410
	I know the seasons, digging, reaping time,	
	Which neither's prayer can alter nor hymn change	
	To fair from evil weather; some there be	
	(Women and some few else) who with good will	
	Lift burden of mass-going: which for us	415
	Makes heavier with but little greater weight	
	The unprofitable necessities of time.	
JOACHIM:	Nay, prayer indeed hath but a human sound,	
	And Innocent who wields it as a law	
	And shield of formal office blunts therewith	420
	The spear of God's intent whose thrust for aye	
	Divides each man from each and all from Him.	
	But yet through prayer for channel drop by drop	
	The slowly oozing waters of man's will	
	May fill the chalice of his being, God	425
	Holds out beneath, until when it be full	

	He lift it to His mouth, against whose lip	
	Water to wine and virtue to desire	
	Flushes in one rare rapture.	

GREGORY: Why, in truth,
There is some profit, for by trick of prayer   430
On which my lord looks favorably, we
May gain a mouth to speak for us with kings.

JOACHIM: Brother, thy words blaspheme! If, as I pray,
The king shall hear you as a voice wherethrough
The eternal manhood of his own heart calls,—   435

GREGORY: It will be long enough before the king
Hear his own heart in any voice save his,
Unless my lord break him with fear of hell.

JOACHIM: I understand not this, ye have learned Christ,
Seen truth, and with me known the things of God: 440
Him dare ye use but as a mask to plead
Demand for temporal benediction? Thou!
Wilt thou make God naught?

GREGORY: In our stream of life
The thought of God is like a rooted weed
Which drags a little at the surface-flow   445
But dams not any current.

JOACHIM: Hath such thought
Less power on man's will than his least desire?

GREGORY: Aye, …that hath touch or thought or may be seen.

JOACHIM: Such bound long since methought ye had outgone.

GREGORY: Living, we may not; dead, perchance, may know   450
If the invisible be and be of worth.

JOACHIM: Ah, brother!

GREGORY: See, I speak but of myself.
                There be amid our village who serve Christ,
                There be who lust for old gods, and there be
                Certain who go in fear of that deceit   455
                Which seems—how oft!—to compass human things,
                Which sometimes in a shudder or the sound
                Of neighbors whispering or a stress of light
                Strains to the very breaking-point of time:
                And others—nay, each man hath dreamed he peered   460
                Over the wall of the world and makes him gods
                Of what he dreamed he saw there; but in truth
                The manhood of all these is more than these,
                For meat and drink are older than belief
                And sleep than faith more needful. So it is   465
                That none have care to stand or fight for thee.

JOACHIM: What gain should I take of your strife? your hands
                Fix fetters on your children's limbs this day
                Which centuries shall not again unloose.
                Ye will not strive? God seeks not for your aid,—   470
                Yet wherefore came ye to the Chapel still?

GREGORY: Custom, or fear, or hope perchance… what else?
                Who knows the way of our hearts' motion?

JOACHIM: God,
                Who as a great sea hides within Himself
                Knowledge of clouds' paths that have being of Him.   475

                                    [*A VILLAGER passes.*

GREGORY [*calling*]: Ho, Gars! I have a word for thee.

The VILLAGER: Speak, then.
                But I must on, …I am in haste: to-day
                My brother's son brings home to him a wife.

GREGORY: I come.
[*To JOACHIM*]:   Is more to say? Think, if thou wilt
                We have not yet learned all that may be taught   480
                Of the gods' kind by our wives' talk, or work
                Of days.

JOACHIM:	Ye will not fight! God's will! again His person yields beneath the Roman's hand, And the first flight of the disciples' feet Patters upon the garden-paths. O Love, Again they come to slay thee in thy thought!	485

                                                                 [*Trumpets at a distance.*

GREGORY: Hearken! The monks! To thee my counsel is,
If any way be open yet, escape!

[*To the* VILLAGER]: Touching the mile of lowland where the kine—

                                                                  [*The two go out.*

JOACHIM:	Flight! Aye, the boy is with me. Michael! For often as by flight God saves man's heart From sin of knowledge, and again returns. Michael!	490
MICHAEL:	What now?	
JOACHIM:	Be swift, follow me in. Thou art more speedy,—thou shalt bear the Thorn. Ah, God, have I been lacking?—we must fly To save it, since the village will not war. With the dim daylight of a mediate sun? Child, thou who hast been fed on holy bread, Hungerest thou now for corn-husks?	495
MICHAEL:	I will out To pluck from danger glory, gold, or song! To gain some great hope, some desire of the world!	500
JOACHIM:	If thou seek empire, there is empire here, And all the circumstance of empire.	
AMAEL:	Ha! Hands spread in prayer shall hardly compass rule.	
MICHAEL:	Nay, he will slip away from thee with words.	505

JOACHIM:	How is it that ye need words? hark, the sea!
	Lo, night! lo, day! how is it that man hears,
	Clinging with Earth to the stillness of God's breast,
	Aught mortal? Or if somewhat thy heart fail,
	Lean back, draw off a little, so to gain	510
	Sight of His face, down-turned to look on thee,
	One thought exchanged betwixt Him and thy soul
	Consummates mediation, holds the strength
	Whence love and rule and all creation is!

AMAEL: Yea, did it strengthen masts and breaking spars   515
       In such a tempest as, off Sicily,
       Held us five days together?

JOACHIM: I that speak
       Knew, when I blest the Cup once, that I held
       Tossing within the circle of the rim,
       In a vision of sound, all sounds that ever were,   520
       The song of birds and poets, roar of crowds,
       Numbers of music, battle-noise of war,
       But rising out of all and over all
       A high-priest calling on a multitude
       And beat of heavy hammers upon nails.   525
       Son, son, where He is, all creation is,
       And there—

AMAEL: Didst thou at that time hear Moire's shout
       When from his foeman's poop he leapt, one arm
       About the bosom of a shrieking queen?
       Or was that sound lost in the voice of Christ   530
       Praying his executioners for wine?
       But shame upon me that I seem to plead!
       Come if thou wilt, young Michael: if not,
       See ships and battles in a cup of wine,
       And dream thou be'st as old as Joachim,   535
       Whose last years well shall with thy young ally.

JOACHIM: Reach forth thy hand to the Maker of the World!
       Son of Christ's passion, turn!

AMAEL: Turn, warriors' son!
       Reach forth thy hand, pluck the world to thy use.

> [*Trumpets at a little distance.*

Hearken, the monks are on thee! choose.

MICHAEL: I choose!   540
Whither?

AMAEL: Go, …take this brooch! …go speedily,
When the monks turn them backward with the Thorn,
Over the hills to the Bay of the White Rocks…
Our ships are there… show the brooch! …Speak of me.
(I come!) to Gorlias! go!

> [*MICHAEL goes out.*

           Ha, Joachim!   545
Let thy god make him friends of older men,
That when he dies they may but for short time
Seek out his grave or mourn above him dead!

JOACHIM: Think'st thou that Christ is as a shipwrecked man
Upon the strange shore of this world, in need   550
Of food, a cloak, and an interpreter,
That for one boy's mock thou shouldst hold him lost?
But O son Michael, thee how many worlds,
How many ages shall down fainter hopes
With heavier vengeance hunt, till thou perchance   555
Poise on the verge of being, whence again
The whole creation's drift may draw thee back
From that edge where is naught save that and thee
On through the circling spheres, till thou at last
Know thyself caught up in the thought of God   560
Where is no time or place but all things are!

> [*He goes again into the Chapel.*

AMAEL: Death is already on thy god: his hands
Pluck at his itch of leprosy, his eyes
Are horrid with the fear of time to come!
O Christ, O Christ, thou art broken, O white Christ!   565

> [*Striking his harp, he goes toward the edge of the cliff. The sound is lost in the blast of trumpets as the ecclesiastical procession appears from the convent path, accompanied by many TOWNSMEN and VILLAGERS.*
> *At the head of the procession are the royal SPEARMEN and TRUMPETERS; then follow the MONKS, chanting, and interspersed with ACOLYTES, THURIFERS, CROSS-BEARERS, and other OFFICERS; the Prior JOHN; then, in cope and mitre, preceded by his cross, the Abbot INNOCENT; CONSTANTINE and his LORDS attending, bareheaded.*]

CONSTANTINE: But art thou sure that there shall be no war?
Hast thou then granted all they sought?

INNOCENT: They deemed
It was our purpose to wall in the hill
And hold this also in our convent grounds.
Which when we swore should be an open place   570
To them for ever, they accepted peace.

CONSTANTINE: There was naught more?

INNOCENT: Sir, naught: what else should be more?

CONSTANTINE: Think not we fear: we hold us bound to keep
The authority of the Holy Father firm
O'er all such fellows as this anchorite.   575
My lord, we so have proved us.

INNOCENT: Doubtless, Sir.
And doubtless God beholds the very heart

Of thy peace, his rebellion, and my deed
Who work this thing to-day betwixt you twain.

> [*The procession gathers on either side the Chapel. INNOCENT, going towards it, meets on the threshold JOACHIM, bearing the Thorn.*

JOACHIM: Hail, Caiaphas! and hail, Pilate! and hail, Jews! 580

INNOCENT: Brother of mine, are yet thine eyes too blind
With sunlight to discern the trodden paths
Whereby we shepherds, though at times our hearts
Forget our master's name, bring sheep to fold?

JOACHIM: That with much thought thou hast in thine own heart 585
Sewn the embroidered vesture of thy might
I well believe: those sandals, wherein shod
Thy stained feet trample on the seamless robe
Have been with casuistry wrought finely out.
And now the last jewel in thy mitre glows, 590
The seizing of the Thorn, the breaking down
Of this last privy garden of God's rest;
That thou again, with hindrance none of men,
May'st speak religious language and make creeds,
Which, that they never should offend Him more, 595
God hushed into the silence of His death!
His thought ye buffet, which He still allows,
Enduring ever through the passionate world,
That which on Calvary broke into our eyes.
This He allows;—take; let me pass!

INNOCENT: Not so; 600
Turn rather thou with us and teach to us,
Who strive and stumble by the holy gate
And hear the oaths and jests of multitudes,
The meaning of archangels' talk within.
Be thou the silence in our midst wherefrom 605
Winds may be loosed of doctrine through the land.

JOACHIM: I have no part in you nor am of you...
Even where these lords and prelates stand I heard

      Immanuel's voice cry like a little child
      Whose mother wrangles in a neighbor's hut.   610
      O the great mother of God is turned aside,
      Earth hath forgot her Son! who now from far
      Calls on all lonely things and calls to me.
      Take thou thy rule to thee for ever. I
      Go forth to follow and find the voice of God.   615

              [*He goes out toward the hills.*

INNOCENT: Benedicat te Deus Omnipotens!
      Brother, my heart is spurned beneath thy foot,
      Yet there is given to me a work, and needs
      Must I thereat still toil.

           [*He turns, lifting up the Crown.*
           The whole assembly fall on
           their knees.

          But ye, draw near!
      Draw near, O poor in spirit! maimed and blind,   620
      Come! and come ye, O little human souls,
      Who are grown miserable in petty sin
      And peevish in small virtue! whose sole breath
      Sighs out, 'Why hast thou thus with me dealt, God?'
      O fools, O sluggards, O faint-hearts, O men,   625
      Come! for again above you in your lives
      That ultimate tradition which is God
      Moves in this creed and law till age on age
      Make of that legend some new human act,
      And act on act through generations make   630
      Earth's air more clear to quiver with that tale.
      So shall men's children 'neath new suns be born
      To new dreams, new deeds; they shall draw great swords
      On evils which men hold not evil yet!
      Out of us poor in spirit shall God make   635
      New earth and heaven; there shall of us be built
      The city whose name is over all names else,
      Rome, Salem, Sarras, Zion, City of God!
      Men's thought shall leave us, and return again,
      Men's hope shall wander from us, and return!   640
      Yea, though all wise, subtle, and holy men,
      For fear of creed, mistrust of government,

     And wrath at the sacrament's being visible,
     Forsake you, be not troubled, but endure!
     Though all the saints desert us, God remains!   645

              [*He comes down from the Chapel.*

     Rise, children! brethren, rise! begin the chant:
     Sing *Regis et pontificis*. Set on.

              [*The procession again forms, and begins to move out.*

The MONKS [*chanting*]:   Regis et pontificit
          Diadema mysticis
            Honoremur laudibus;   650

THEODORIC [*to a LORD, passing out*]:
     A time shall be when we will break this man,
     And all the treasure he hath gathered up
     Into his convent shall become our own.

The MONKS [*chanting*]:   Jocundemur tropicis,
          Canticit angelicis   655
            Concordemur moribus.

JOHN [*passing out*]:   Children, kneel down when the Lord Abbot comes.

CONSTANTINE [*passing out*]:
     I shall be boasted over all old kings
     Because I have set Christ above all gods.

The MONKS [*chanting*]:   In corona Domini   660
          Forma datur homini
            Pulchre necessaria;

INNOCENT [*passing out*]:
     Lift up your heads, O gates! be lifted up,
     O everlasting doors! your King comes in.

The MONKS [*chanting*]:   Spina mortis stimulus,   665
          Sed coronae circulus
            Mortis est victoria.

[*The procession passes from sight. Some VILLAGERS follow it; many remain.*

GREGORY: We too can sing. Come hither, Amael:
Make music for us here.

AMAEL: What shall I sing?
Wilt thou I call upon the Fire of the Wild 670
Or the immortals?

GREGORY: Thou shalt not sing of gods.
Sing us a tale of Druhild.

The VILLAGERS [*speaking confusedly*]: Aye, well said.—
My father told of him when I was young.—
Knowest thou not he shall return again
To drive out strangers?—Aye, my grandsire's tale.— 675
Sing thou of Druhild, him who yonder sleeps.

AMAEL: Make then a place that I may set my foot
Within the holy Chapel of the Christ,
And ye shall have such singing as ye will.

[*He passes through the VILLAGERS into the Chapel.*

The MONKS [*chanting at a little distance*]:
Honc coelorum Rex portavit, 680
Honoravit et sacravit
Suo sacro capite;
In hac galea pugnavit
Cum antiquum hostem stravit
Triumphans in stipite! 685

[*AMAEL, standing within the Chapel, has begun to sing. A few of the VILLAGERS take up and answer his song.*

The VILLAGERS: Lord of the marshland and the wood,

>   Who came in darkness and in blood,
>   And smote the high kings where they stood,
>   Druhild the folk-lord, hail!

GREGORY [*to The First VILLAGER*]:
>   What does yon woman on the edge of the crowd   690
>   Who seems as if she prayed upon the ground?

The First VILLAGER:
>   Let her alone: she deems her son is healed
>   By one god or another; let her be.
>   I am sure my grandsire of such sickness died.

The MONKS [*chanting in the distance*]:
>   Jesu pie, Jesu bone,   695
>   Nostro nobis in agone
>   Largire victoriam;
>   Mores nostros sic compone,
>   Ut perpetuae coronae
>   Mereamur gloriam.   700

AMAEL [*playing and singing*]:
>   Then Druhild stood among his men,
>   The tallest by a span;
>   Weapons are here at choice (he said),
>   For the hand of every man.
>   Spears have they taken from us,   705
>   That their use may be forgot,
>   But clubs we knew of olden time
>   When spears and swords were not!

The VILLAGERS [*all shouting or singing*]:
>   Lord of the marshland and the wood,
>   Who came in darkness and in blood,   710
>   And smote the high kings where they stood,
>   Druhild the folk-lord, hail!

The WOMAN: And let thy blessed hands make whole in him
>   All sickness in his days! in life and death,
>   O Mary, Mother of God, be pitiful!   715

Notes

Epigraph: The editor has supplied the Scripture reference.

Dramatis Personae: The words "Dramatis Personae" are the editor's addition. Furthermore, none of the characters' names appear in all caps in Williams's MS; the editor has added those.
CONSTANTINE: See the introductory essay for a discussion of the historical identity of this character called Constantine.
INNOCENT, Abbot of the Monastery of St. Cyprian: Here the original reads "Cyprians," but CW crossed out the "s."
AMAEL: The original reads only "a singer"; the rest is the editor's addition for clarification.

Setting: The word "Setting" is the Editor's addition.
St. Cyprian. There was a real, historical St. Cyprian: "Thaschus Cæcilius Cyprianus," Bishop of Carthage in the third century.

Act I

Stage Directions: Throughout the manuscript, CW underlined words that he wanted to appear in italics, especially stage directions. However, these lines were not underlined; the editor has placed them in italics to conform to other stage directions elsewhere and has made similar changes for consistency silently throughout.

2-3. Notice the syncretism in these lines: line 2 refers to candles in the Christian chapel, while the "five-cornered shape of stones" refers to an occult pentagram. For a discussion of Williams's hermeticism, refer to the preface and introduction.

4. The original line read "Frighten bad spirits further from men's tombs." This is CW's revision. From this point on in the endnotes, all revisions are CW's unless identified otherwise.

6. The original line read: "If thou at all canst hope aught helpful from this god."

15. The original line read: "That slew both Andreas and his chamber-maid."

26. After this line, there are six lines are crossed out with two large diagonal slashes:

>   The First MAN: There will be strife between that Abbot soon
>   And we of the houses on the lower shore,
>   For he is bent to make this Chapel his,
>   Chapel and land.
>   The Second MAN: And build a wall about?
>   That shall not be till Druhild from his tomb
>   Rises, or we are slain there.
>   [*A monk passes: the two step aside.*
>   The MONK: Benedicite!
>   [*He goes out.*
>   The Second MAN:

35. CW revised "to day" to "this day."

38. CW changed "e" to "i" in pencil in order to change "the" to "this."

39. Again, CW changed "e" to "i" in pencil in order to change "the" to "this."

41. It is difficult to determine whether the third word in this line is "hight" or "night"—whether the villager is swearing by Druhild's name or by the night that is associated with him (see the note on line 135, below).

54. "Benedicite! pax tecum Domini!" is "Bless you!" or "Be blessed! The peace of the Lord be with you!" Thanks are due to Andrew Lazo and Gavin Ashenden for their assistance with translation.

63. CW changed "pray" to "fast."

74. CW changed "sailed" to "gone."

76. On the blank page facing this one, the word "blest" is legible half-way down in the left margin in Fred Page's handwriting; this probably means he was querying the scansion of "Blessed" (which could be read as two syllables), suggesting "blest" instead, since that would obviously scan as one syllable.

93. CW changed "offering" to "offerings."

116. On the facing blank page, Fred Page penciled in an "X" here, with the comment "*I can't make this line scan—only, at least, by accenting ban**ner** [stress mark] which is ugly ? 'bannered Cross.'*"

117. Revised from "Till the great day whereon their last high chief."

130. The word "burn" is written in a second time in pencil above the inked original and circled, probably as a clarification of the unclear handwriting.

135. Here ten lines are marked for deletion with three diagonal slashes:
                    To keep the land, the Chapel, and the Thorn!
    Amael: Thou! fight to keep the memories of the Christ!
["the" appears to be crossed out twice: once in pen, once in pencil]
    Gregory: Hark, when the first priest, Cyprian, when he
                   Who bore this Thorn (their talk!) of the Death of the God
                   Built up this Chapel, stablishing the watch
                   Of three priests by it, in our fathers' time,—
    Amael: The gods are angered with us for their sake:
                   They should have slain him then!
    Gregory: Upon whose tomb
                   Built he the Chapel?
    Amael: The altar thereof stands
                   Over the hidden place of Druhild, he
                   Called also Of the night and Of the Trees.
    Michael: Is it for that the shoremen came to watch,
[there are marks correcting "shoreman" (singular) to "shoremen" (plural)]
                   While here is Mass sung, round about the door,
                   But come not past the threshold?
    Amael *[crossed out]*: Gregory: Thou hast said.

136. Revised from "Content we were to watch and wait, but now."

139. Revised from "About it: then shall no man this plot of land, till none shall more go in,".

146. CW changed "of" to "from."

168. The word "since" is added below "months" with a bracket, because it did not fit on the same line of text. This occurs in many subsequent places throughout the MS, but they are not noted in the rest of this edition.

177. In this line, "Who therefore left his father's gods," the "s" in "father's" and the "s" in "gods" appear to be crossed out.

199. Here "in" has been crossed out and replaced with "to."

204. CW began to write a word here, but crossed it out right away (judging by the ink, which appears the same as the rest of the poem) and wrote "mouth." Based on context and on the ascender at the beginning of the crossed-out word, the editor speculates that he was going to write "breath."

216. CW crossed out "in" and replaced it with "to" before "youth."

226. Notice the similarity of this line to the Fairy's lines in *A Midsummer Night's Dream* (II.i.2-7):
>Over hill, over dale,
>Thorough bush, thorough brier,
>Over park, over pale,
>Thorough flood, thorough fire,
>I do wander everywhere,
>Swifter than the moon's sphere….

and the devil's claim in Job 1:7 (NIV): "The LORD said to Satan, 'Where have you come from?' Satan answered the LORD, 'From roaming through the earth and going back and forth in it.'"

243. CW crossed out "Yet" and replaced it with "But."

248. The "h" of "him" is triple-underlined, as if either CW or Fred Page wanted it capitalized; however, other pronouns referring to Christ are not usually capitalized throughout this text (but see note 28 below).

275. This line originally read: "To ~~no man~~ none on earth will I give up the Thorn."

289. On the blank page facing this one, Fred Page made a note in pencil about half-way down, near the left margin: *"A thought in a shaft? feather."* He seems to be asking whether this image, of a thought in a shaft, is a mixed metaphor.

291. "To-morrow is Saint Cyprian's day" recalls Ophelia's "To-morrow is Saint Valentine's day" in *Hamlet*, Act IV, scene 5, line 47.

319. Notice this inconsistency as regards the capitalization of pronouns referring to God.

330. There was an ellipsis after "Peace, Peace!" with a squiggle over it, which the editor has read as a mark of deletion.

333-4. A large double bracket }{ connects these two names, suggesting that John and Joachim speak at the same time.

337. There was a comma after "nay," but CW crossed it out.

340. There was a squiggle over the first ellipsis in this line, which appears to be a mark of deletion, but the editor has chosen to preserve it.

351. The word "one" has been crossed out in pencil after "If" and the word "ye" has been added in pencil.

357. CW changed "the" to "thy" in pencil.

361. Here "s" is struck through in pencil to change "dares" to "dare."

362. Again, "s" has been struck through in pencil to change "dares" to "dare."

370. Notice the metrically curtailed line, which may perhaps be for emphasis.

381. Notice another rare instance of a metrically incomplete line.

384. "Deposuit!" Immediately before this line, Innocent has commanded his monks to sing the *Magnificat*: Mary's song after the Annunciation, which begins "My soul doth magnify the Lord: and my spirit hath rejoiced in God my Savior." The word "Deposuit" begins a later section of the *Magnificat* in Latin, which praises God because "He hath put down the mighty from their seat." In context, this is a subtle but effective insult to Theodoric: a claim that sacred power is greater than his secular force.

389. On the facing blank page, Fred Page made a note in pencil about half-way down, near the left margin, reading: "*Is this a formal authentical curse? No: ~~the d~~ it is a scientific statement.*" The word rendered "authentical" here is difficult to read, as are the crossed-out letters. "Authentical" is the editor's best guess, although there appears to be a dot above the "e," as if it is an "i." Others are welcome to play hangman with Fred Page and come up with an alternate reading.

394. This line begins "Threaten's men's sin" in the MS. The editor has changed it.

401. Here "manner" has been crossed out in pencil and replaced with "measure."

420. Here a whole line has been crossed out between lines 420 and 421; it read: "And common custom of ancestral time."

422. Here four lines have been crossed out between lines 422 and 423; they read:
>   Such use, subordinate ever to new law.
>   Nor yet do we interrogate the claim
>   My lord Theodoric makes; if he speak truth,—
>   The Justicer is servant of the law,

The two central lines, from "Nor yet" to "speak truth," are marked for deletion with a diagonal slash.

423. There was originally a period after "All law"; CW changed it to a semi-colon. Also, the "W" of "wherein" is struck through in pencil, indicating a change from uppercase to lowercase.

433. After "his servants," the following words have been crossed out:
>   on to sacrilege, who fain
>   Would have dragged off a man from holy place;
>   I accuse him of

Then the word "to" has been inserted; this inserted word and its attendant caret, written in pen, are penciled over again, perhaps to make sure it is not overlooked.

436. The word "the" originally appeared after "Against," but is doubly crossed-out in pen, then violently scribbled over in pencil.

437-8. These two lines have been crossed out, but then "Stet" is written in pencil in the left margin by these two lines, indicating that they should be left in.

443. After line 443, twenty lines have been marked for deletion with a diagonal slash. They read:

>   Need is not that thou shouldst at all repeal
>   License or grant, which in thy sovereignty
>   Have their interpretation. Let thy word,
>   Ensceptered over spear and pastoral crook,
>   Stablish a new law in a final court;—
>   Choose fine among thy princes unto whom
>   May be appeal from monk's or warrior's word
>   By whom in either argues an offense.
>   Theirs to determine jurisdiction, draw
>   Tables of precedent and count of crime
>   Which in its proper hour and place, for cause
>   Allowed by law, may flee to sanctuary.
> Constantine: Well hast thou said; and, cousin, first shalt thou
>   Bring question to our such court of privilege,
>   Even this same matter of thy vassalry.
> Theodoric: Choose rather me among the judges, king.
>   Since need were not that I should question them
>   If...
> Constantine: Thou, my lord the Justicer, shalt draw
>   The parchments. Since to-morrow is the feast
>   Of holy Cyprian, on the after day

Within those lines were a few other small corrections, which are not noted here.

443-4. These lines have been significantly altered. First, two lines have been deleted. They read:

>   The court shall hold its session...
> Innocent: Yea, so soon?
>   Let me have place to speak another words.

Then "Nay, let me yet hold place for other" has been written in above the line it corrects, "Stet" is written in pencil above "yet" to clarify that it should not be deleted (although it is not crossed out), and the "s" of "words" has been added in pencil.

447. "Judges" crossed out and replaced with "princes."

450. Several lines have been deleted after line 450:

>   This new-made court I contradict, deny
>   Its jurisdiction, and reject its rule.
> Theodoric: Ha, rebel!
> A Lord: Thine allegiance to the king
>   Wilt thou deny?
> Innocent: Allegiance? Let the king
>   Hear me, the abbot, not the Justicer.

451. This line went through several revisions to make it fit with the deletion above.

453. This line is squashed between those preceding and following it, suggesting it was added later, but in the same ink (so at the time of copying, rather than the time when the penned corrections were made).

462. CW started to write "proper," then changed his mind and wrote "such" (apparently noticing the word "proper" in the previous line and seeing that a monosyllable scanned better).

466. CW crossed out "whereof" and replaced it with "of what." Fred Page queried this line, asking if it should be: "*of what He make't*".

468. There are several changes to this line, thus: "Thou hast no need of Church or priesthood more: Thy land word." Then an entire line was deleted below it, which read: "Is thy heart sure? Thou art the king;".

471. A comma has been crossed out and replaced with a period. "Send" was also originally capitalized, because "To" was added later.

472. One line has been deleted and another altered. The original line read: "To ~~And~~ govern all this people as thou wilt." Then CW crossed out "To," and finally ended up writing this new line: "To Send ~~some one~~ one man of all these, ~~to~~ and forbid".

489. The "e" of "Sayest" is crossed out, making the final reading "Say'st."

Stage Directions before line 490: The word "others" was originally capitalized. About this stage direction, Fred Page asked: "*Were they indeed so unanimous? even in the outer ring*" and CW replied: "*No, but those who spoke were.*"

492. This is difficult to transcribe: there are two periods, the second of which is crossed out, underneath an em-dash. It appears that CW wanted his unique period-dash combination.

493. Here "cities" is written darkly over some other, illegible, word.

541. CW crossed out "impeach" and replaced it with "accuse."

545. Here "d" has been added in pencil to change the word from "free" to "freed."

549. At the beginning of this line, "On them" has been crossed out and replaced with "Upon."

562. CW crossed out "That" and replaced it with "Which" in the margin in pencil.

563. CW wrote in an editorial mark to indicate he wanted to switch the word-order; it originally read: "'Twixt such necessities the choice is be theirs:—".

583. There is a dash crossed out above the ellipsis in this line.

617-8. Amael's lines, "Have ye no need to be baptized of me, / That I should come to you to be baptized?" are a parody of Matthew 3:14. Jesus comes to John the Baptist for baptism, "But John tried to deter him, saying, 'I need to be baptized by you, and do you come to me?'" (NIV)

632. "Surely" is written over (or possibly under) another word, which is indecipherable.

633. An entire line has been crossed out before this. It read: "A stray man and a schemer, an outlaw." Thus the present line 633 is a revision of that deleted line, and contains several revisions: "A~~ A Stray, ~~and~~ a reckoner-up of ~~men,~~ lands, ~~houses, flocks,~~ men, herds,". There is a further note by Fred Page that seems to suggest "herdsmen" instead of "men, herds."

634. CW changed "thereof" to "whereof."

646. Here "them" has been corrected to "there."

664. The word "to" has been deleted after "raise."

Stage Directions before line 673: CW deleted the word "deep" after "returns."

690. CW crossed out "Songs" and replaced it with "Chants."

693. Fred Page queried whether there should be a comma after "O" at the beginning of this line.

694. Fred Page queried whether this line should end with a question mark.

705. Fred Page queried this line, suggesting "As on what altars…"

706. Here "human" has been crossed out and replaced with "mortal."

708. Here "mortal" has been crossed out and replaced with "human."

731. This originally read "God's"; the deletion of the apostrophe-s seems to introduce pantheism into Joachim's beliefs.

732. CW replaced "And" with "Yea" at the beginning of this line, and also added a comma in pencil after "will."

733. Here "the" has been crossed out and replaced with "my."

736. There is a note by Fred Page suggesting "? *(intervening)*?" It may refer to the end of line 732 or the dash in line 736, as both have pencil marks.

741. CW crossed out "soul" and replaced it with "heart."

748. Here "hope" has been crossed out and replaced with "way."

759. A comma has been crossed out at the end of this line.

766. Fred Page wrote a comment on the facing sheet asking: *"But has Amael any hope. this seems rather pure worship as of Juggernaut."*

760. A comma has been crossed out at the end of this line.

775. A comma has been crossed out at the end of this line.

787. Here "about" is written in over another, illegible, word.

793-4. Fred Page wrote a note asking: *"Do you want the italics? or quotations"*.

Stage Direction after line 794: "In" crossed out and replaced with "After."

800. This line contains several changes, thus: "We, ~~have grown~~ being fearful, ~~and~~ do of late neglect". Fred Page recommended this emendation of the line: *"Which . . (we have grown fearful) we neglect"* and added a nearly illegible comment that says something like: *"(O Mrs. Samp!)."*

Stage Directions after line 800: "slowly" has been doubly crossed out here after "turns then."

809. Here "voyager" has been crossed out and replaced by "sojourner."

825-27. "The keys of heaven and hell" is a quote from Matthew 16:19. It is part of Jesus's words to Peter, on which the Roman Catholic Church partly bases its teachings related to the establishment of the papacy. In connection with "Sword of Saint Paul," it appears that Joachim is accusing Innocent of an extremely power-hungry, militant Christendom.

831. A variety of editorial marks show that CW considered three versions of this line:
    1) Here then let my voice meet with equal voice
    2) Here then with equal voice let my voice meet
    3) Let then my voice meet here with equal voice.
The last version appears to be his final intention.

835. The names were originally reversed in this line: "What say'st ~~thou, Joachim, of me, Innocent?~~ of Innocent, thou, Joachim?"

842. This line originally read: "Baptizing them by names of Faith and Love."

846. This line originally read: "But knows not behind what shut door it grows." Fred Page asked: *"? can a tree grow behind a <u>door</u> Why not beyond?"* CW took his advice and altered the MS accordingly.

855. Joachim claims that Innocent has made "Religion" into "a fair for kings," which may be an allusion to Vanity Fair in *Pilgrim's Progress* by John Bunyan.

856. This line contains several revisions: "And ~~used~~ bred the soul of man ~~for~~ to market-drudge."

857. This line contains several revisions: "And ~~doth~~ keeps she not ~~keep~~ her house within the world? . . ."

873. Fred Page wrote a note comparing this to a line of poetry by Alice Meynell: "*Cf. Mrs. Meynell Intro to C. P. Muses' L. p. 13 — 'As an incommunicable planet'—!*" The editor believes that Page is referring to the book *The Angel in the House together with The Victories of Love* by Coventry Patmore, which was published in The Muses' Library series by E. P. Dutton & co. in 1905 with a seven-page introductory essay by Alice Meynell.

892. This line contains several revisions: "~~Bar of the Church's~~ Doctrine and bar of dogma, at his side."

911. This speech was originally given to Joachim, but CW crossed out that name and gave it to John.

914-17. These lines originally read thus:
> Against thy will and name who art come down,
> Armed with the spearmen of the king, and with
> Commission and authority from Rome
> To hold above the faithful judicature?

before CW revised them to the present version.

949. The parentheses, "(I speak as a fool)," is a quotation from 2 Corinthians 11:21, when Paul breaks into his own chain of logic to say "—I am speaking as a fool—." This line also includes an allusion to Joel 2:28: "And afterward, I will pour out my Spirit on all people. Your sons and daughters will prophesy, your old men will dream dreams, your young men will see visions," which is quoted in Acts 2:17: "In the last days, God says, I will pour out my Spirit on all people. Your sons and daughters will prophesy, your young men will see visions, your old men will dream dreams." (NIV)

957. CW corrected "his" to "His"—but notice that pronouns referring to God are not standardized in this text.

962. Here "Gather" has been crossed out and replaced with "Rally."

963. CW revised "paramour" to "adulterer."

966. CW changed "e" to "i"—to change "the" to "this"—in pencil at the beginning of the line. Also, a circle and line indicate that "wholly" should be moved, resulting in a final version of: "Till this world's axis wholly hath been changed!" There is a note that may suggest Fred Page wanted to retain "Till wholly this world's axis hath been changed!"

976. Here "thou" originally occurred after "wilt," but has been crossed out.

Stage Direction in line 997: CW began writing some word beginning with "o" (possibly "out"), then changed it to "up."

1008. A comma has been crossed out after "stood up," and another at the end of this line.

1013. This originally read "In parting and the gathering."

1025. On the previous sheet, Fred Page asked "*Why time?*" It is a good question; one would think "steps" or "speed" or even "feet" would make more sense for a lame man.

Act II

2. Fred Page queried the capitalization of "Them," noting especially the discrepancy between the Villager and Amael. There was also originally some inconsistency in the Villager's capitalization, which the editor has rectified.

11. The line contains several revisions: "Is peril in ~~of~~ Their malice ~~and~~ toward my harm."

19. "These" is written over another word that appears to read "These" also. In addition, the MS read "when thou," which does not make sense, so the editor has emended it to "whom thou."

20. "Art friend to" has been crossed out and replaced with "Befriendest."

22. "Which" has been crossed out and replaced with "Whither."

29. There is a penciled "X" at the end of this line. The editor has been unable to determine what it signifies.

36. Here "drink" has been crossed out and replaced with "meat."

39. A comma has been crossed out at the end of this line.

61. A comma has been crossed out after "labour."

63. The editor has added a comma at the end of this line.

72a. Fred Page wrote a note questioning the repetition of "else" in the first half of this line. Also, this line originally contained two commas, thus: "Yet one, who was high-priest ere I,".

101. Here "of" crossed out and replaced by "from."

105. This line is squashed in between those that precede and follow it. Also, the colon at the end is partly crossed out, suggesting it could be amended to a period.

110. "Earth" in this line was originally lowercase.

117. The MS read "the harp-bearer," and the editor has emended this to "thy harp-bearer."

Stage Direction after line 148: Here Fred Page underlined "ill" "Hill" and "hill" and wrote *"ill hill hill"* on the blank facing sheet, pointing out that this was an overemphasis on internal rhyme.

154. Notice the metrically curtailed line.

155. The editor has added an ellipsis after "strange," as it appeared to have no punctuation in the MS.

156. This originally read: "womens," but CW corrected it.

159. This line originally read: "Still pray to them when keen eyes only serve." Fred Page wrote: "'*serve*' here will imply, to the listener, '*serve the gods*'." CW took Fred Page's advice and emended to "will suffice."

174. This line originally read: "I told him naught he had not guessed before."

179. A period is crossed out at the end of this line.

185. A period is crossed out at the end of this line.

188. A comma is crossed out at the end of this line.

193. This line contains many revisions: "~~About~~ Around the ~~door~~ door-posts to ~~look upon~~ behold his tomb."

194. "No" has been crossed out and replaced with "none."

206. Here CW first forgot to tab over the line of text (in order to preserve the metrical divisions), but then remembered, crossed out "Look" with a double strikethrough, and began again.

213a. "Wherefore wouldst" has been crossed out and replaced with "Why wouldst thou" written in above the crossed-out words.

228. This line contains several revisions: "~~So have w~~We promised, so, and so will we perform:"

228-230. Notice the slant rhyme of "perform" and "Thorn"—one of the few instances of rhyme in this play.

233. Here "old" is added in pencil.

234. An indecipherable word is penciled in above "Teach." "Man" was originally "a man."

235. Originally "?.?" but the second question mark is crossed out.

237. Again, this was originally "?.?" but the second question mark is crossed out.

242-43. Notice the similarity of these lines with the epigraph.

254a. "Shalt" is crossed out and replaced with "Mays't."

255. This line originally read: "Thou wouldst have women to thy lust? And he," but CW changed it to read "Thou lustest after women? And thy lord;". There is also a crossed-out letter "T" following "after." In addition, the editor has changed the semi-colon to a comma.

262. Here CW changed "holds" to "thinks."

267. Here Fred Page wrote a note: "*cf Joachim at foot of p. 21 / So you intend Amael / dramatic truth all taught / in this way?*" And Williams wrote in reply: "*Yes why not?*" Page appears to be referring to Joachim's claim: "Yet all we / Teach the Lord Christ" (I:250-1).

293. Here "blood" has been changed to "soul."

300. At the end of this line, either Fred Page or CW crossed out the end quote; the editor restored it.

343. Fred Page asked, "*Are the gates 'galleries'?*"

344. The final rendering of this line is difficult to determine. As it stands in the MS, it reads: "(High-galleried in) Beaten + fashioned, through cause and consequence,". "Beaten + fashioned, through" is in pencil, as are the parentheses, leading the editor to the reading in the present text. Furthermore, Fred Page suggested: "*in cause and consequence to?*"

345. "Up" has been added at the beginning of the line, leading the editor to give "to" a lower-case "t." Also, "the" is circled, possibly as an indication of deletion.

350. Here there is a circled plus mark; its significance is unknown to the editor.

352. CW originally had "president," but crossed that out and replaced it with "consular."

364. This line originally read: "For ever, when (thou knowest their story) he", but CW changed it to: "For even, when he—thou hast heart their tale—".

366. Here CW changed "He fashioned dust" to "Dust-fashioned he." The editor has removed the hyphen, because it seemed to confuse the meaning.

368. "Which" changed to "This."

385. Here CW changed the lower-case "h" to an upper-case "H."

389. The question mark at the end of this line is involved with another character, whether correcting or being corrected is unclear.

390. CW changed "peril" to "danger."

392. This line begins with a crossed-out "Y," as if CW was going to begin the line with "Yet" instead of "But."

404. This line originally read: "Of Him, the primal and eternal Act,".

421. Here Fred Page underlined "ay" and wrote on the facing blank page: "*aye*." The editor has taken the liberty of applying Page's correction.

422. "Defends" revised to "Divides."

432. CW added an "s" to change "king" to "kings."

456. Here "full" has been revised to "how."

466. Fred Page wrote on the blank sheet facing these lines: "*Isn't this rather metaphysical for a villager?*"

476. The last letter of this character's name is difficult to read; it may be Gare, Gart, or Gars....?

480. CW altered "learned" to "taught."

498. Here "That" is doubly crossed out here and replaced with "Child."

499a. An apostrophe in "hungr'st" is crossed out in pencil and an "e" written in below, so that the final reading of this word is "hungerest."

533. This line seems to indicate, by its scansion, that "Michael" is pronounced in the Hebrew fashion, with three syllables.

536. Here "years suit" has been crossed out and replaced with "ally."

538. CW changed "warrior's" to "warriors."

547. There is a comma here, crossed out, after "dies."

555. Here CW began to write "perchance thou," but then reversed the words.

559. There is a "p" crossed out before "circling."

595. Here CW changed the lower-case "h" to an upper-case "H."

601. This line originally read: "But rather turn with us and teach to us,".

612. Here CW revised "whose" to "who."

625. An exclamation point has been crossed out and replaced with a comma at the end of this line.

640. An "s" has been crossed out to change "wanders" to "wander."

647. "Regis et pontificis", etc. This hymn is taken from a poem wrongly attributed to Adam de Saint-Victor, entitled (fittingly), "De Corona Spinea," "Of the Crown of Thorns." Here is the text as Williams has rendered it, with an English translation by Digby S. Wrangham. Many thanks to Andrew Lazo for discovering this source and translation for me.

Regis et pontificit	Let us to high honour raise
Diadema mysticis	In glad strains of mystic praise
Honoremur laudibus	Our High-Priest and Monarch's crown
Jocundemur tropicis,	And, while we in tropes delight,
Canticit angelicis	As we in their songs unite,
Concordemur moribus	Make the Angels' life our own.
In corona Domini	For the chaplet of the Lord
Forma datur homini	Doth a needful type afford
Pulchre necessaria	To mankind most happily;
Spina mortis stimulus,	Its sharp thorn is death's sharp sting,
Sed coronae circulus	But the round encircling ring
Mortis est victoria	Of that crown death's victory.

[here Williams omits four stanzas from the version printed in Wrangham's edition]

Honc coelorum Rex portavit,	'Twas the King of heaven wore it;
Honoravit et sacravit	Since His sacred temples bore it,
Suo sacro capite;	Great and holy must it be:
In hac galea pugnavit	In this helmet He contended,
Cum antiquum hostem stravit	When the old foe's sway He ended
Triumphans in stipite!	By that triumph on the Tree!
Jesu pie, Jesu bone,	Good and gentle Jesu! hear us!
Nostro nobis in agone	In our conflict be Thou near us,
Largire victoriam;	That we may full victory share:
Mores nostros sic compone,	Guide our lives so, we implore Thee,
Ut perpetuae coronae	That we ever *there* before Thee
Mereamur gloriam.	Glory's deathless crown may wear!

Richard Sturch also provided me with his own prose rendering:

> Let us praise and honour the crown of our King and High Priest; let us be happy with music in harmony with the angels' songs. In the Lord's crown a beautifully necessary form is given to man. The thorn is the sting of death, but the circlet of the crown is the victory of death. The King of Heaven has worn it, honoured and sanctified it with His holy head. It was the helmet He wore when He defeated the ancient enemy, triumphing on the Tree. Kind Jesus, good Jesus, grant us victory in our battle; so shape our lives that we may be worthy of the glory of an eternal crown.

651. Here and elsewhere, "passing out" does not mean "fainting," but "exiting."

657. Here "bow" has been revised to "kneel."

663-4. This is a quotation from Psalm 24:7 (or Psalm 24:9, which repeats the refrain), which the NIV renders as: Lift up your heads, you gates; be lifted up, you ancient doors, that the King of glory may come in."

673. CW changed "way" to "was."

691. There is a note here on the blank facing page, crossed out, that appears to read "*preyed upon*," as if Fred Page misunderstood CW's intention.

698. "Mores" is written over an illegible, crossed-out word.

715. At the end of the MS is written in Fred Page's handwriting: "*Gibbon – Vol 3.*"

APPENDIX

The Chapel of the Thorn
An unknown dramatic poem by C. Williams [1]

In September 1924, Humphrey Milford decided for the OUP that *Outlines of Romantic Theology*[2] was "not for us", and Charles Williams, in reporting this in his letter of the sixth to J. D. C. Pellow, wrote: "So the unfortunate *Romantic Theology* shall cuddle the equally unfortunate *Chapel of the Thorn* in a private seclusion."[3] Was it a seclusion so private as to make this mysterious *Chapel* like "the fatal and fascinating Q which no man has seen at any time but the contents of which we so neatly know" (HC 60)[4]? It was not. For *The Chapel of the Thorn* emerged from its seclusion to be read by Pellow, who wrote in his diary for "July 3rd" 1925, "transcribed passages from Williams's Chapel of the Thorn. A dramatic poem rather than a poetic drama; the characters are types or embodied attitudes. The Abbot Innocent perhaps the most living figure. The various attitudes (Ioachim—the pure mystic + anarchist; Amael the pagan mystic; Gregory, the 'natural man', the Prior John—the mere ecclesiastic—naked authority; and Innocent—authority tempered with wisdom + vision) are well + sympathetically set forth, and, at times, in what magnificent poetry,—e.g. Amael's speech about the Gods,[5] and Innocent's final call to the Poor in Spirit[6] … 'Though all the saints desert us God remains'"[7]. But what then?

In 1969, the late Professor Sir Fernando de Mello Moser wrote of the *Thorn*: "provàvelmente, foi destruido",[8] confessing "Ignora-se o que sucedeu ao original"[9] (284). And in her *Exploration*, Mrs. Hadfield speaks of "the lost *Chapel of the Thorn*" (39), saying "John Pellow gave me eight pages of extracts which he had made [...] These pages in my possession are all that seem to remain of the work" (238). And the rest … is happily *not* silence. For, on that significant day, 1 April,[10] in 1942, Raymond Hunt got a revised authorial holograph of "The Chapel of the Thorn: a Dramatic Poem"[11] from Williams via Margaret Douglas. And he passed it on, with so many other Williams papers in his possession, to Wheaton College, where, in the Marion E. Wade Collection, it has at last emerged from private seclusion.

Moser dates *The Chapel* c. 1923 (76, 284). Mrs. Hadfield says Williams "finished a play and sent it to John [Pellow] on 10 May 1924 saying 'nobody loves it (except me)', asking for his opinion on the theology rather than the verse. He tried to turn the manuscript from a two-act into a one-act piece and messed it up. Is this, perhaps, the lost *Chapel of the Thorn*?" (*Exploration*, 39). But the holograph is clearly inscribed "C. W. Augt. 24/12". Whether the work referred to in Williams's letter to Pellow of 10 May 1924 is *The Chapel*, whether Williams revised the "Dramatic Poem" in the twenties, and whether what Pellow transcribed from was the extant holograph, I do not know, as I have not yet had the opportunity to collate Pellow's transcriptions with the MS., or to reread the letter of 10 May, since reading the poem. But whatever Williams was doing with *The Chapel of the Thorn* in 1924, he had certainly written it by August 1912, and that makes it, so far as we know, his second major work. But that fact is only the beginning of its importance.

In Williams's first major work, *The Silver Stair* (written c. 1908-09, published 1912), there are other characters than the poet-Lover: it is seeing the "elect" "servitors of Love" (sonnet 5, l. 1) which helps stir him to seek "Love" (sonnets 1-7). There are references to "them of the king's household" (sonnet 45, l. 7), among whom he is numbered, and to Love's "goodly company" (sonnet 68, l. 3); and, as Dr. Cavaliero has observed, *The Silver Stair* is full of "Images relating to the City".[12] But these are not developed, or even individualised, human characters, nor are the entities represented by those words so significant in Williams's late Arthurian poetry ("household" and "company") explored; and the images "relating to the City" are not images of the city as an organic community. Even where different responses to the possible or actual experiences of "Love" are exemplified by different characters (as in the sestet of sonnet 5, and especially in sonnet 51), those characters are merely examples of responses, and are invisible otherwise. In sharp contrast to this is the first page of the Arthurian Commonplace Book (probably begun c. 1912 or after), where characters from the Matter of Britain are linked with different kinds of love. What seems to have occurred between the two is *The Chapel of the Thorn*.

In *He Came Down from Heaven*, Williams, looking at "the progress of the tale" (23) of the Bible, speaks of the story of Cain and Abel as "the opening of the second theme of the Bible—the theme of *pietas* and the community." (22). And, of the transition from what he calls "The first book, as it were, of the myth" to "the second" (23) after the introduction of this "second theme", he says: "The very style of the Bible itself changes; the austere opening pulsates with multiplied relationships. Man becomes men." (24). I would suggest that this is a truer characterisation of Williams's own development, from *The Silver Stair* to *The Chapel of the Thorn* and the proposed Arthurian epic, than of the first six chapters of Genesis. From the almost solely-developed character of the poet-Lover, whose various responses or potential responses to experience—especially the experience of "Love"—are minutely studied, and who is himself, internally, the *locus* of most of the significant action of *The Silver Stair*, Williams turns to the many distinct characters Pellow enumerates, and to the violent clashes of them and their ideas. "Man becomes men." And "the community" becomes a centre of attention. This is not surprising, since Williams is turning from a sonnet sequence, "a form", C. S. Lewis says, "which exists for the sake of prolonged lyrical meditation" (EL, 327)[13], to a "Dramatic Poem". But it is not insignificant either. Not only does *The Chapel of the Thorn* provide the first real examples of Williams's attention to "the City", but ideas evoked by that image are central to the work.

First, however, let us attend to Pellow's insightful description of "the characters" as "types or embodied attitudes". Rather than being entertained in the mind of one lyric persona, attitudes are embodied in—or as—characters and clash in a drama. We might compare Williams's comment on the characters in Blake's Prophetic Books—"individuals in his verse [...] are only there to reveal the states of being in which they exist" (FOS 92)[14]—and apply it to his own work (substituting "largely" for "only"). *The Chapel of the Thorn* is the first example of the attitude toward, and use of, characters, which mark Williams's subsequent fictions, especially the novels.[15] In some works, a peculiar symbolic nature of the characters is explicitly pointed, as in T*he Rite of the Passion*, where "Love" calls the disciples

> twelve foundation stones of man
> at his creation builded into place,
> [...] twelve principles of grace

and says of the Virgin Mary

> Yet have I one is mightier than all these,
> who are her children and capacities;
> [...] she is the soul that is chosen to be the mother of me.[16]

Such examples raise questions about all his characters, but we cannot here pursue the fascinating subject of Williams's characterisation.

However much, and in whatever way, they are "types" or symbols, the characters of *The Chapel* are all sufficiently "living figures" that one is concerned about their development and the choices they may and do make. It is choices and dispositions respecting the Hallow of the title—significantly, like the Grail and the Spear of Longinus, a Hallow of the Passion—which give rise to the action of the poem. The work is not, however, as Moser plausibly conjectured, concerned with the legends of Joseph of Arimathea and Glastonbury (284-85), though, as we shall see, there are flashes of the Matter of Britain, and a more than passing relation to Williams's handling of it.

Chapel and Thorn are in the keeping of the eremitic priest, Joachim, who would prevent their coming under direct control of the Church hierarchy, whose representative the abbot Innocent is. Joachim hopes the local people, his flock, will defend the Chapel, by force if necessary, unaware of the extent to which they are in fact crypto-pagans and interested in it primarily as a pagan holy place, the tomb of the divine (or divinised) hero, "Druhild, he Called also Of the Night and Of the Trees", and elsewhere "called the Slayer of Kings" (Amael, 14, 80),[17] whose return they await. They are consequently quite willing to allow the Thorn to change hands. The poem is set at a significant moment in time, for the one clearly historical character in it is the Emperor Constantine, who enters near the end to say "I shall be boasted over all old kings / Because I have set Christ above all gods" (102).[18] I have not found definite sources for other characters or names, though it is possible that "Amael" recalls Amergin of the *Lebor Gabála*;[19] and that Williams is practicing the kind of play with near—(and not-so-near—) contemporaneity that he contemplates in the Commonplace Book, and Innocent is to be identified as he who became Pope Innocent I (AD 401-17). It may be, as well, that the opposition of the eremitic contemplative, Joachim, and the abbot Innocent is meant to recall those of Joachim of Fiore (or his followers, and their teachings) and Pope Innocent III.[20] The clash of "attitudes" which embroil communion and community, not only have theological dimensions which are recognised by characters, but are often explicitly clashes of "theologies" or metaphysical worldviews (as well as of "mysticisms").

The mass of common people merely want to get on with their accustomed lives (cf. the Chorus in *Murder in the Cathedral*). Gregory, a villager leader and a crypto-pagan, in reporting to Joachim that no one will fight to keep the Thorn, says

	Few men shall hold a danger ["peril"] to their souls
	Worth peril of their bodies to prevent.
Joachim:	But know they not how small thing all else is?
Gregory:	Small! it is that we know we have,—a hut,
	Talk with our kinsmen, wife or chamber-maid
	To keep the hut, a sleeping-place, and food.
	Small! it is that we have.
Joachim:	And they are ways
	Whereby the soul aspires to God, whom won,
	Except for his sake they are no more worth
	Than candles burned out in solemnities
	Which Innocent the Abbot makes for God.
	All doing is but littleness to them
	Who, even as we, are, of His favour, ware,
	By intellectual vision, mental sight,
	Of that One ["Him, the"] primal and eternal Act,
	Immanent and transcendent, wherein shine,
	Co-equal, co-eternal, consummate,
	All purpose and all process and all end! …
	Whereof is contemplation our best deed. (86)[21,22]

Joachim declares a "sacramental" or significant order in the universe, and, for all his individualism, a hierarchy of importance, displaying Gregory's "goods" and "ends" as means to an all-embracing End.

Amael, with Joachim and Innocent one of the three main protagonists, self-proclaimed as "a singer, a minstrel of the gods, A priest in mine own office" (43),[23] unlike the mass of pagan or crypto-pagan commoners, is a mystic and, as it were, a theologian. The theology he presents is like a kind of Hinduism:

> There is a darkness beyond all the gods,
> Where once in many ages That which Is [,]
> In Its eternal sleep whose dreams we are [,]
> Heaves suddenly and shudders half-awake.
> […] the All-being moves,
> And all the visible and invisible worlds
> In that sole motion ruin and are re-born
> Into fresh lands, new nations, other gods. (50-51)[24]

Later, contending with Innocent, he rehearses his "knowledge" in terms of mystical experience (anticipating Williams's use of the Taliessinic poetry):

> Nay; I was old in that ere he was born.
> I know the forest-paths, I know the caves
> Whence the first men crawled, with lean hands that clawed
> Like the wild beasts they learned their hunting from!
> I know the smell of blood upon the track
> Where first men snarled above the prey 'lo, mine!' [...]
> And all the treacheries of the warring worlds!
> I have gone down and in a dark night laid
> My hands upon the leash of that desire
> Which evermore the gods let loose on us,
> And felt about my brows the wind-like lust
> That blows to changing shapes this mist of men! (80-81)[25]

The "he" of the first line quoted seems from the context to refer to Christ (and "that" to "the folklore of the world" which Innocent equates with "Christ, [...] that word [...] His name; wherein all thoughts of Druhild move" (80)[26]). The first six lines seem to present his knowledge in terms of some mysterious direct vision of the prehistoric world in the first ages of man. The last five lines seem to describe a mystical descent. The first description is in terms of evolutionary commonplaces, the second is mythic. But both are concerned with desire, seen as basic, inherent, and selfish, always giving rise to strife.

Both of Amael's speeches present a perpetual process arising from the activity of something impersonal and not fully conscious. The second shows an immanent "lust" or "desire" "Which evermore the gods let loose" driving the universe. In the first, Amael goes beyond his usual polytheism to some sort of impersonal pantheistic monism. There is no intention here, just a dreaming and half-awaking with the creation or annihilation of worlds on worlds as by-products. Here is the theme of "a new heaven and a new earth",[27] but with a newness that is no renewal: there is no perfection or redemption, only arbitrary monotonous repetition. While "desire" is not mentioned, selfishness is implied: "That which Is", "the All-being" is a careless solipsist. One might say that there is no Reason in Amael's worldview, only Will. Man is both to some extent destined to be selfish, and foolish to attempt to be anything else. There is a suggestion that man might master the driving force "of the warring worlds": "My hands upon the leash of that desire". But the end of that also is mere annihilation: in fact, a characteristic modern view.

However much Joachim and Innocent may differ, they agree in opposing to Amael's view a more inclusive one which features a more comprehensive understanding of "desire". What Amael considers ultimate—self-interested desire—is shown as partial and rudimentary. To Amael's teaching concerning "desire"—"Women for love, vengeance for hate: what more?"—Joachim responds "Such loves and hates are as the firstling flames / Which crackle through life when the torch of birth / Quickens a man's will into fire for God." (21)[28]. He sees not only the common needs and objects of desire as ways to God, but the very desire for them—and even for vengeance and hate—as symptomatic of growing desire for God.

And when Innocent's saying "the Faith is older than all men" elicits Gregory's objection "Yet none among our fathers know thy Faith",[29] Innocent responds-using and varying the same imagery as Joachim:

>   All men have known it as some ancient thing
>   That chanced to them or mayhap to their sires.
>   And had thine own no tales for drinking time?
> Gregory: Stories of heroes and of kings at war.
> Innocent: And therein was a torch lit, though it threw
>   But red light, dim with smoke and blown with wind,
>   Where the wise pagans lit their vestal lamps,
>   Wherewith the candles on our altars burn,
>   At fire upon all household hearths, the light
>   That lights all men who come into the world,
>   The Christ that was born man before man was.
>   [...]
>   Therefore, there never was nor ever shall
>   Be meeting under any moon or sun
>   For a god's worship or a hero's tale.
>   But therein higher hymn and history
>   Surge and become tumultuous in that flood
>   Of waters loosened from the inland hills. (81-83)[30]

Near the end of the poem, Innocent says

> That ultimate tradition which is God
> Moves in this creed and law till age on age
> Make of that legend some new human act,
> And act on act through generations make
> Earth's air more clear to quiver with that tale. (100-01)[31]

—lines which seem to anticipate the speeches of Cranmer and members of the Commons in Cranmer (26-27, 41-42)[32]: there the English Bible, here "creed and law" and "legend", form "a sacrament of the Word". The exemplary and formative is to be acted upon—there, providing "a strong order, a diagram clear"—or in some sense enacted—here, "age on age / Make of that legend some new human act". He presents a progressive, reciprocal dialectical process between "the tale" and human action which in some sense purifies the world.

But while Innocent would relate human desires and acts—and legends and stories—to God, he would not do so indiscriminately. After Amael's speech about "desire", Innocent says to him

> Thou hast gone near the making of the world.
> Yet of that old forgotten legendry,
> Those whispers of the flesh and soul ["blood"], those lusts
> In passages of blood or thought, those dreams,
> Those hauntings of our fathers in ourselves,

> No voice, save of the Church, hath will to choose,
> Knowledge to safeguard, strength to overthrow.
> No voice but hers alone decrees aright:
> *This is a rumour of religion; that,*
> *A slander breathed by Satan out of hell.*
> So wise she is, so pitiful, so stern,
> Because the Faith is older than all men. (81)[33]

And so to the exchanges with Gregory quoted above.

He makes the point as strongly when the "second villager" says

>   Joachim then lied,
> Teaching that God was in our midst and all
> Desire was from him and toward him at last?
> Innocent: Son, thou hast heard amiss.
> Villager 2:   Mayhap. I heard
> Joachim teach that only a man's will
> Must be the rule and measure of his deed,
> That by his doing what he would to the height
> Should he find out the… God.
> Innocent: And if he taught
> That thou shouldst only work thy wicked will
> He taught a damnable heresy, as thou
> May'st ["Shall"] find, in hell. […]
> Thou lustest after women? And thy lord,
> ["wouldst have women to thy lust? And he,"]
> Theodoric, would slay men at his will,
> And the king grind the poor to gain more gold,
> All so to live their lives out and find God! (78-79)[34]

It does not seem the villager grossly misrepresents Joachim here. Innocent is the advocate of tradition and "the dusty ground of common law" (79)[35] and the authority of the Church, while Joachim says "Let rather men be bold to sin then be / O'erruled by terror" (49: a deliberate echo of Luther?)[36] and "In each man's separate being God is judge" (24)[37], and asks "Are not these poor folk whom God died for, free / From any law except Christ's pulse in theirs, / And singularly his in each one beats." (29).[38] Their differences are well shown in two exchanges:

(1)

> Innocent: Must each man learn the dialects of God
>   Not as a child learns, being taught, but as
>   The whole world stumbled slowly into speech?
> Joachim: Is not each man a new world before God,
>   […] alone,
>   As any incommunicable star?

Innocent: But what love is that is not in itself
Absolute law? which law, made visible,
Audible in the advent of God's self
(Whereof we are the echo through the years)
Is the direction and control of man. (56-57)³⁹

(2)

Innocent: What wilt thou? wilt thou teach these village-men
The mystery of this, Love's sacrament,
Yet, till their lives have learned that First and Last,
Alpha and Omega of God's ways with men,
Deny to them the single certain way
Of learning such dear wisdom, in the life
That treads, though hardly, with shut eyes, the Law?
Joachim: Save a man's will be gained, his life is naught.
Innocent: Nay, by life only shall a man's will learn. (61)⁴⁰

Both seem to see the good as the gaining of "man's will" by God, so that self-centered desire is put away and one's will moves at the direction of the Divine love. But they disagree as to how this is to be brought about. Innocent remarks to John

> Joachim
> Hath seen, and follows that he saw till death.
> He with all saints may climb high paths, [...]
> [...] breathe
> The chill air of supernal Thought⁴¹

but, describing themselves as "we, Who hold the monstrance of the common heart," says "the lesser man shall conquer, …even I." (62).⁴²

The "sacramentality" of the creation and the possibility of knowing—or beginning to know—"the Faith" without being aware that it is "the Faith" you are knowing, and the need to choose, and to know, rightly, are illustrated in the subplot concerning the apparently minor character, Michael. Michael is Joachim's young companion. But his father was a pagan, who, Amael says to Michael, "Learned song and journeying and sorcery, / As thou, his son, might'st learn of me" (69).⁴³ His character, the way that he will go, is not settled. We might say, indeed, that he is the first of the young people who are not so obviously tending one way or another and who seem especially faced with a significant choice, which characterise Williams's fictional works (most notably the novels)—unless the Lover in *The Silver Stair* is the first. Like the Lover he sees around him others who have chosen, whom he may imitate or follow, though unlike the Lover and the later young people he is not obviously at the centre of the work.

A conversation about him shows him to have suffered and to suffer (and develops the theme of organic relation which is the seedling of Williams's doctrine of human co-inherence, and has a hint of the latter's cognate doctrine of "exchange"):

> Gregory: he bears
> The times of twain his brethren, they who died
> In the great plague, last followers of his creed.
> Amael: Do his eyes grow more dim that theirs are shut,
> Or his limbs weaken because theirs are still?
> Gregory: Nay, yet their hands pluck at him from their grave. (15)[44]

Early in the poem, he reveals his restlessness and impatience with the life of religious discipline, saying

> I am weary of these prayers and hymns
> And mysteries of the holy bread and wine,
> And spiritual visions to be seen
> In due time, if I fast and watch the Thorn! (9)[45]

Part of Amael's temptation is something Michael already desires: he wants to travel to lands which have

> All men and things!
> Ports where a thousand ships may ride at ease,
> And markets of sweet perfume; images,
> White stone and purple,—iron-caged animals,
> Flat scaly fish as long as thirty spears,
> Lions caught in the desert,—sun-stained palaces
> Whose stairs are lit as if upon each wall
> Innumerable altar-candles burned,—
> Kings who have black men for their cup-bearers,
> And yellow-featured slant-eyed slaves for guard (10).[46]

And, at last, he does choose "journeying". But his seeking of "All men and things!" and his speaking of stairs lit as if by "Innumerable altar-candles" suggest that the cities of his dreams are images of "the City" and his desires for them "the firstling flames" quickening his "will into fire for God", which may lead him at last to seek and find "spiritual visions" "Of that One primal and eternal Act, Immanent and transcendent". Unbeknownst to himself, he is a pilgrim. He is in some sense exercising "will" rightly, rightly desiring the good, without knowing it. But this does not mean he does not need correction and direction, or that he is not erring, as well as seeking, in ignorance. And it is Joachim who recognises and proclaims this, when in a speech both sorrowful and hopeful, he says

> But O son Michael, thee how many worlds,
> How many ages shall down fainter hopes

Appendix   131

> With heavier vengeance hunt, till thou perchance
> Poise on the verge of being, whence again
> The whole creation's drift may draw thee back
> From that edge where is naught save that and thee
> On through the circling spheres, till thou at last
> Know thyself caught up in the thought of God
> Where is no time or place but all things are! (96)[47,48]

Joachim and Innocent, then, seem agreed that love must be set in order, goods preferred to evils, and higher goods to lesser ones. And, even more than in *Shadows of Ecstasy*, it does not seem immediately obvious where Williams's own sympathies chiefly lie. With their conflict, Williams raises issues of central concern to Christianity—for the last five centuries at least—and not to Christianity alone. As Pellow says, "the various attitudes [...] are well + sympathetically set forth", vividly and grippingly. And it is not surprising that he provides no satisfying, convincing solution. But I think Williams's sympathies are with Innocent, and the evidence for this, and perhaps something of an implied solution, lead us to "the image of the City".

Rome is a powerful image here, and is seen within the poem as such. Amael wonders

> through what might can one small city's name
> Outdo her arms in power on utmost shores
> Till the extreme lands round about the world
> Seem but the lower slopes of seven mounts
> Upon whose pleasant inner side is Rome? (69-70)[49]

And when Innocent has proclaimed the value of all meetings "For a god's worship or a hero's tale", Amael asks "What matter then if thou should teach or I, Because all teachings are of equal worth?"[50] To this, Innocent responds

> Who hath supposed them so? What mind hath trod
> To equal profit either thought of twain?
> Or what blurred eyes have held the reedman's hut,
> Poor and alone in robber-haunted fens,
> More meet for all men's dwelling than that town
> Which now is built and building, where through gates
> High-fashioned through ["-galleried in"] cause and consequence,
> To the aerial certitudes of thought
> Squares of broad virtues are, wind-swept by grace,
> And streets made wide in vows and marriage-loves
> 'Neath pediments of temples virginal,
> And conduits running Eden-streams, but wine
> On city-feasts, and each way going up
> To the open space of the Forum, where all hearts
> Are citizen to the consular ["president"]-heart of God,
> Where justice is—of just men's brotherhood,
> Freedom, and safety of all conscious things,

> Closed in these white republican walls of Rome …
> Whereto, O God, a little let me toil! (83-84)[51]

And toward the end of the poem Innocent develops the imagery further:

> Out of us poor in spirit shall God make
> New earth and heaven; there shall of us be built
> The city whose name is over all names else,
> Rome, Salem, Sarras, Zion, City of God! (101)[52]

Both these speeches, like Joachim's concerning "that One […] Act", stress comprehensiveness, the many in one, the second by the paradox of "The city whose name" being followed by the names of four cities.

And this urban imagery is paralleled to some extent by organic or body imagery. Amael says, in apostrophe to Innocent, "Wilt thou have all men in thy city, monk? There shall be yet some few who ride without." (85)[53] While Joachim begins by asking:

> Wilt thou do hurt? shall the hand smite the head?
> Shall the foot bruise its fellow, wherethrough smote,
> Even as through thine, the nail that pierced the Christ,
> When all of us in Him were crucified? (27)[54]

but ends, after having lost Thorn, Chapel, and Michael, by saying to Innocent "I have no part in you nor am of you …" (99).[55]

One is reminded of Williams's "one dichotomy", (IC 113),[56] what Pope Deodatus, in "The Prayers of the Pope", is willing to consider the "difference" between those marching on the Empire and those in it:

> If there be difference, it must be in thy sense
> that we declare […]
> and they deny […]
> that we derive from them and they from us,
> and alive are they in us and we in them. (ll. 94-89; RSS 48)[57]

Amael and Joachim reject or deny their "member-ship", attempt to keep aloof or to detach themselves from the whole which comprehends them. Innocent, by contrast, repeatedly proclaims comprehensiveness—even grouping Joachim "with all saints". He guards and declares the "common"—the rich multiplicity of meaning of the word dances before us.

The solution I suspect to be implied, is some sort of grounding of right and right judgement in this comprehensive view, though, if so, I do not see that it is a solution. Unfortunately, it does not seem that Williams has attempted to imagine convincingly how "No voice, save of the Church, hath will to choose, Knowledge to safeguard".[58]

It will have been noticed that among the cities named by Innocent, casually classed with "Rome", "Salem", "Zion"—apparently as names of the "City of God"—with no further explanation, is "Sarras".[59] This is tantalising. The context here suggests the significance, and weight, Williams already accorded "Sarras". But how much does this lone, somewhat intrusive reference imply? How extensive and settled was Williams's "reading" of the Grail story already by August 1912? And how much was the single word "Sarras" intended to convey: were the whole story of the quest and an interpretation of the quest poised on this?

It is not the only hint of Williams's handling of the Matter of Britain. As a transcendent comprehensive Eucharist has already been central to *The Silver Stair* (see sonnets 15 and 79) so in *The Chapel of the Thorn* Joachim recalls a mystical vision of all creation which befell him at a Eucharistic consecration:

> I that speak
> Knew, when I blest the Cup once, that I held
> Tossing within the circle of the rim,
> In a vision of sound, all sounds that ever were,
> The song of birds and poets, roar of crowds,
> Numbers of music, battle-noise of war,
> But rising out of all and over all
> A high-priest calling on a multitude
> And beat of heavy hammers upon nails.
> Son, son, where He is, all creation is,
> And there— (94)[60]

Another comes when Joachim charges Innocent with abusing prayer in imagery reminiscent of the Grail Hallows:

> Nay, prayer hath but a human sound,
> And Innocent who wields it as a law
> And shield of formal office blunts therewith
> The spear of God's intent whose thrust for ay
> Divides ["Defends"] each man from each and all from Him.
>
> But yet through prayer for channel drop by drop
> The slowly oozing waters of man's will
> May fill the chalice of his being, God
> Holds out beneath, until when it be full
> He lift it to His mouth, against whose lip
> Water to wine and virtue to desire
> Flushes in one rare rapture. (87)[61]

The images of the thrusting of the spear and the filling of the chalice are not explicitly linked: but they are formally linked by the consideration of the function and use of prayer. And the sequential juxtaposition recalls both the traditional image of the blood from Christ's side being caught in a chalice, and the depiction of the Grail procession in some romances.[62]

Someone (as yet unidentified) to whom Williams had shown his Commonplace Book has written in it, "Certain stories are quite absent from your notes—e.g. Balin + Balan". This occurs after Williams is well-along in his notetaking and pondering: on page 128 (so, after October 15, 1914).[63] Fourteen pages further on (142), Williams asks in reference to "the 'dolorous stroke': does this mean the use of sacred things for 'temporary' ends—the use of personality (created by the Eternal Generation) for its own purposes, personality guarding itself in its own selfhood, instead of yielding itself completely up?—as Balin used the lance for his own welfare". This symbolic interpretation of the Hallows and this reading of the incident of Balin at the Grail Castle is adopted (see IC, 175)[64]. Balin is linked with Arthur (e.g., CB 151), and this link and the parallels between their acting from a " 'self-hood' motive" are developed in the Arthurian poetry.

Whether this interpretation of the Hallows and "the dolorous stroke" had occurred to Williams before he noted it in the Commonplace Book, we do not know. But the theme in some form is central to *The Silver Stair*. And the imagery is certainly anticipated here. What Joachim accuses Innocent of is twisting prayer, which should be directed to the service of God, to try to blunt "God's intent". But, as suggested earlier, the theme is found not only in such a detail as this, but seems a concern of the whole work.

When Joachim asks Innocent "Wilt thou do hurt?" he refers to the Crucifixion (27)[65]; and he does so again when he accuses Innocent, saying "His thought ye buffet, which He still allows, / Enduring ever through the passionate world, / That which on Calvary broke into your eyes". (99)[66] Innocent, in his turn, exclaims to Joachim, "War! *Thou*—thou wilt use / Evil to conquer evil?" (41)[67] The Thorn, like the Spear, is an engine of the Passion. But where Balin wields the Spear to wound again, here violence is threated to secure the Thorn. It seems to be implied that to use violence to secure a Hallow is to misuse your powers and to be improperly disposed toward It. It is to misunderstand the significance of the Hallow: to misunderstand the Crucifixion.

Amael delights to mock at the apparent weakness of Christ. He asks, "Shall thought of Druhild, called the Slayer of Kings, Seek grace from thought of Christ whom such kings slew?" (80),[68] and interrupts Joachim's account of his "vision of sound" in "the Cup" with

> Didst thou at that time hear Moire's shout
> When from his foeman's poop he leapt, one arm
> About the bosom of a shrieking queen?
> Or was that sound lost in the voice of Christ
> Praying his executioners for wine? (94)[69]

But the Chapel of the Thorn stands, significantly, over the tomb of Druhild. Druhild has not risen again. His tomb is not in that sense empty. And though the pagans wish and hope for his return, rather as Roger Ingram does for the return of Considine at the end of *Shadows of Ecstasy*, we do not expect it. The "ways" of Druhild and Considine are seen to be insufficient, and therefore false, ways, however much their partial truth and considerable appeal are recognised, however much they are "shadows" of the whole truth. (Cf. Adam-Augustus in *Seed of Adam*.)

The Suffering Servant is Christus Victor, kenotic in His victory. His saving act is one of obedience, submission, self-emptying. The action is Passion. And the Thorn is a Hallow because of this kenosis, and a witness to, and a memento of it, and a call to its imitation. It is a relic of the action by which God atones (at least potentially) all to Himself and each other. For professed Christians to fight each other over—or with—relics of the Passion is therefore heavy with a grim irony. What testifies to atoning suffering is made a cause of inflicting division.

And it is here that the "'selfhood' motive" and the selfish misuse or assertion of "personality" comes in. Constantine, in his farcically ironical brag, "I shall be boasted over all old kings / Because I have set Christ above all gods",[70,71] reveals himself as, in effect, a king after the order of Druhild. And Amael's philosophy of selfish desire, and perhaps Joachim's radical individualism, as well as their rejections of the "city" and their "member-ship", can be seen as examples of the "'selfhood' motive" in action, and of the misuse "of sacred things".

There is much that must be passed over entirely, and much else that has had to be barely presented without examination in so brief an introduction as this. And among what has been passed over are some things which make one uneasy and call for criticism. These include signs of Williams's speculations about extra-temporal or counter-sequential activity, which are connected with that preoccupation with a "timeless eternity" already clearly revealed in some of the passages quoted above. For example, after Innocent's visionary description of "Rome", Gregory says to Amael

> I have heard him say,
> Preaching before the king upon a feast,
> That, since God acts not many times but once
> For ever, when he —thou hast heard their tale—
> ["(thou knowst their story) he"]
> Worked wood in Nazareth, to those who saw
> He fashioned dust to stars and clay to men,
> Wherein all those who labour have their part:
> This ["Which"] I remember for that afterwards
> Old Andreas the carpenter, who died,
> Laughed at his toil, swearing he made the worlds.[72]

To which Amael responds "Nor lied he, if thine Abbot did not lie." (84).[73] And there is Joachim's apparent pantheism and his exaltation of the "will", the latter of which Williams seems to endorse in the Commonplace Book:

> [...] where one beast, one stone is, God is there.
> His will and man's will are; and what more powers
> He hath created to free use of will
> Have therein separate being; save for this,
> There is naught of matter or spirit but God,
> Yea ["And"] all man's being, save his will, is God. (49)[74,75]

But perhaps there is enough here to show that *The Chapel of the Thorn* is not only of considerable historical interest as a milestone in Williams's literary and intellectual development, but quite interesting in its own right. It is, as Pellow says, "A dramatic poem rather than a poetic drama", though it ends with the strikingly theatrical effect of monks chanting "Regis et pontificis" alternating both with various bits of dialogue, and with a song of Druhild sung antiphonally between Amael and the villagers (102-105). But while we may never see it produced as a play (though even that would be interesting), might we not hope with some realism that it will one day come even further out of its seclusion, perhaps in an edition of Williams's *Complete Dramatic Works*? It is well worth reading, and deserves to be more widely known. [76]

—David Llewellyn Dodds

---

[1] Editor's note: This article by David Llewellyn Dodds was first published in the *Inklings-Jahrbuch* 5 (1987), pp. 133-152. Copyright © David Llewellyn Dodds 1987; used by permission. The present text is a transcription without editorial changes; this means that any variations in quotations from the play are preserved as they appeared in the 1987 text.

[2] Editor's note: Works cited may be found in the bibliography at the end of the current edition.

[3] Author's note: C. W. to J. D. C. Pellow, 6 Sept. 1942. Quoted (with a slight variation) in Alice Mary Hadfield, *Charles Williams, An Exploration of His Life and Work* (NY 1983), 45. I wish to thank Dr. and Mrs. R. J. N. Pellow for their great hospitality and kindness, and their permission to quote from J. C. D. Pellow's writings, and especially Dr. Pellow for magnanimously on his own initiative searching his father's diaries for references to C. W. to aid my researches. The published works of this neglected poet include *Parentalia and Other Poems* (London 1923) and *Selected Poems: George Every, J. D. C. Pellow, S. L. Bethell* (London 1945); he is also represented in Norman Nicholson's *Anthology of Religious Verse* (Harmondsworth 1942).

[4] Williams, *He Came Down From Heaven*.

[5] Probably I:750-66.

[6] II:619b-45.

[7] II:645.

[8] Author's note: *Charles Williams: Demanda, Visão e Mito* (Lisboa 1969), 76.

[9] Editor's note: This translates roughly to "Probably, it was destroyed," and "it is not known what happened to the original." Thanks are due to the friends who discussed this quote on social media.

[10] Author's note: Cf. "The Founding of the Company", ll. 111-53, RSS, 37-38; and the unpublished poem "1 April, 1938", which exists in several forms, and refers to the publication of TTL: my thanks to Mrs. Thelma Shuttleworth for suggesting this context for this poem. Editor's note: the poem "1 April, 1938" may be found in a MS entitled "Amen House Poems" at the Marion E. Wade Center as CW / MS-27.

[11] Author's note: MS. title. My notes are from a clear photocopy of the MS. rather than the MS. itself. I am grateful to Dr. Lyle Dorsett, and all the staff of the Wade Collection, and to Wheaton College, for allowing me to see this photocopy, and for all their kind help with my researches, and their hospitality.

[12] Author's note: Glen Cavaliero, *Charles Williams: Poet of Theology* (London 1983), 13.

[13] Editor's note: Lewis, *English Literature in the Sixteenth Century*.

[14] Editor's note: Williams, *The Forgiveness of Sins*.

[15] Author's note: And one might say his critical approach to characters as well; cf., for example, *Reason and Beauty in the Poetic Mind*, (1933), chapters 8 and 9.

[16] Author's note: In *Three Plays* (1931), 146-47. And cf. Williams's adumbration of "twelve-fold personality" in *Outlines of Romantic Theology*, first footnote of chapter 2 (page 24 of the extant TS). Editor's note: In the published edition of *Outlines of Romantic Theology* (see bibliography), this quotation occurs on p. 21.

[17] Editor's note: Dodds is using the page numbers in the MS. For this quote in the current edition, see I:40, the note on I:135, and II:269.

[18] II:658-59.

[19] Editor's note: The *Lebor Gabála Érenn* is mythology or pseudo-history, and contains poems attributed to the bard Amergin. The reader is referred to Charles Squire's *The Mythology of the British Islands* or *Celtic Myth and Legend*, which discusses similarities between poetry attributed to Amergin and to Taliesin (pp. 123-24).

[20] Author's note: I am very grateful to Dr. Marjorie Reeves for discussing this aspect of the poem with me, but accept full responsibility for the use I have made of her information and suggestions.

[21] Author's note: Where C. W. has revised the text, I give the final reading followed by the earlier reading in square brackets. Editor's note: Quotes are given here exactly as they appeared in Dodds's 1987 article. See the introduction, text, and endnotes of the present edition for further discussion of revisions.

[22] II:390-408.

[23] I:621-22.

[24] I:758-61, 764-66.

[25] II:277-82, 285-90.

[26] II:271-75.

[27] Editor's note: Revelation 21:1.

[28] I:256, 258-60.

[29] II:302, 303.

[30] II:304-14, 330-35.

[31] II:627-31.

[32] Editor's note: Williams, *Thomas Cranmer of Canterbury*; p. 18 in the edition on the current bibliography.

[33] II:291-302.

[34] II:244-58.

[35] II:263.

[36] I:739-40.

[37] I:316.

[38] I:545-47.

[39] I:868-73, 882-86.

[40] I:984-92.

[41] I:1013-17.

[42] I:1017-18, 1028.

[43] II:79-80.

[44] I:156-61. Editor's note: In context, it becomes apparent that these lines refer to Joachim, not to Michael.

[45] I:64-67.

[46] I:78-87.

47 II:553-61.

48 Author's note: This speech, like T. S. Eliot's "On the edge of a grimpen" (*East Coker*, l. 91), seems to recall Francis Thompson's "Hound of Heaven". The imagery of falling should be compared with "Richmond Park", PoC, 18; Barbara's experience in WH, chapter 13; Giles Tumulty's in MD, chapter 16; Wentworth's dream and the end of DH; and "Taliessin on the Death of Virgil", TTL; and the salvific meeting with Barbara's, and with Taliessin's poem. Editor's note: the works by Williams referred to in this note are: *Poems of Conformity, War in Heaven, Many Dimensions, Descent into Hell*, and *Taliessin through Logres*.

49 II:92-96.

50 II:332, 336-7.

51 II:338-56.

52 II:635-38.

53 II:372-73.

54 I:356-59.

55 II:607.

56 Editor's note: Williams, *The Image of the City*.

57 Editor's note: Williams, *The Region of the Summer Stars*.

58 II:296-67.

59 II:638.

60 II:517-27.

61 II:418-29.

62 Author's note: And cf. "Taliessin's Song of the Myths" in the largely unpublished *Advent of Galahad* cycle (c. 1930) (which I am editing as an appendix to my dissertation). Editor's note: I am happy to report that David Dodds published many of the *Advent of Galahad* poems in his edition in Boydell's *Arthurian Poets* series (see the bibliography at the end of the current text). The poem in question occurs on pp. 174-6.

63 Author's note: I am also editing the Commonplace Book (hereafter CB) as an appendix to my dissertation. Editor's note: Alas, the *Commonplace Book* has not yet seen publication—but there is hope that it may yet do so, in the very near future.

64 Editor's note: Williams, *The Image of the City*.

65 I:356.

66 II:597-99.

67 I:583-84.

68 II:269-70.

69 II:527-31.

70 Author's note: Cf. CB, 9: "Constantine's fault […] the abandonment of the last forms + pretences of the Republic; the beginning of admitted tyranny."

71 II:658-59.

72 II:361-70.

73 II:371.

74 I:727-32.

75 Author's note: In CB, on 109, in a discussion of "will", "wills", and the Hypostatic Union in the context of Lascelles Abercrombie's remarks on *Paradise Lost* in *The Epic* (1914), Williams writes, "But how do two wills exist in one being? 'what more powers He hath created to free use of will Have therein separate being.' If we are nothing but wills, how had Christ two, yet one person?"

76 Author's note: All quotations from the published and unpublished works of Charles Williams are [©] Michael Williams 1987. I would like to thank both Mr. Williams and Mr. Bruce Hunter and David Higham Associates Ltd. heartily for their very generous permission to quote from Williams's work so extensively, especially from his unpublished works. Their kind permission does not, of course, imply any endorsement of my interpretations or opinions. Any factual errors are also my own.

Bibliography

Ashenden, Gavin. *Charles Williams: Alchemy and Integration*. Kent State UP, 2007. Print.
Brewer, Elizabeth. "Charles Williams and Arthur Edward Waite." *VII: An Anglo-American Literary Review* 4 (1983): 54-67. Print.
Carpenter, Humphrey. *The Inklings: C. S. Lewis, J. R. R. Tolkien and Their Friends*. New York: HarperCollins, 2006. Print.
---, *W. H. Auden: A Biography*. London: Faber and Faber, 2011. Print.
Cavaliero, Glen. *Charles Williams: Poet of Theology*. Grand Rapids, MI: Eerdmans, 1983. Print.
de Saint-Victor, Adam. *The Liturgical Poetry of Adam of St. Victor: From the Text of Gauthier with Translations Into English in the Original Meters and Short Explanatory Notes by Digby S. Wrangham*. Vol. 3. London: K. Paul, Trench, 1881. *Google Books*. Web. 5 Jun. 2014.
de Troyes, Chrétien. *The Complete Romances*. Trans. David Staines. Bloomington: Indiana University Press, 1993. Print.
Dodds, David. "Another Constantine!" Message to Sørina Higgins. 6 April 2014. E-mail.
---, ed & intro. *Arthurian Poets: Charles Williams*. Rochester, NY: The Boydell Press, 1991. Print.
---, "Re: Concerning the relevant relic." Message to Sørina Higgins. 4 April 2014. E-mail.
---, Introduction to Charles Williams's *Arthurian Commonplace Book*. Unpublished.
---, "Some notes on names in The Chapel." Message to Sørina Higgins. 4 April 2014. E-mail.
Dunning, Stephen M. *The Crisis and the Quest: A Kierkegaardian Reading of Charles Williams*. Carlisle, Cumbria: Paternoster Press, 2000. Print.
Edwards, Diane. "Christian Existentialism in the Early Poetry of Charles Williams." *VII: An Anglo-American Literary Review* 8 (1987). 43-57. Print.
Eliot, T. S. Introduction. *All Hallows' Eve*. By Charles Williams. Vancouver: Regent College Publishing, 2003. Print.
The Emerald Tablet of Hermes. Trans. Madame Blavatsky. *Sacred Texts.com*. Web. 9 June 2014.
Geoffrey of Monmouth. *The History of the Kings of Britain*. Trans. Lewis Thorpe, 1966. NY: Penguin, 1996. Print.
Gilbert, R. A. *A. E. Waite: Magician of Many Parts*. Bath, UK: Crucible, 1987. Print.
---, *The Golden Dawn: Twilight of the Magicians*. Aquarian Press, 1983. Print.
Gildas. *On the Ruin of Britain (De Excidio Britanniae)*. Trans. J. A. Giles. Rockville, MD: Serenity Publishers, 2009. Print.
Hadfield, Alice Mary. *Charles Williams: An Exploration of His Life and Work*. Oxford UP, 1983. Print.

Hallowell, John H. *Modern Canterbury Pilgrims and Why They Chose the Episcopal Church*. New York: Morehouse-Gorham, 1956. Print.

Harris, Micah, and Michael Gaydos. *Heaven's War*. Berkeley, CA: Image Comics, 2004. Print.

Higgins, Sørina. "Double Affirmation: Medievalism as Christian Apologetic in the Arthurian Poetry of Charles Williams." *Journal of Inklings Studies* 3.2 (2013). 59-96. Print.

---, "Is a 'Christian' Mystery Story Possible? Charles Williams' War in Heaven as a Generic Case Study." *Mythlore* 30.115/116 (2011): 77-90. Print.

Higgins, Sørina and Rebecca Tirrell Talbot. " 'Between Two Strange Hearts': Spiritual Desolation in the Later Poetry of Gerard Manley Hopkins & Charles Williams." *Inklings Forever* VIII (2012). May 31 – June 2, 2012. Taylor Univ. The 8th Francis White Ewbank Colloquium on C. S. Lewis and Friends and the C. S. Lewis and the Inklings Society Conference. 64-72. Print.

Hopkins, Lisa. "Female Authority Figures in the Works of Tolkien, C. S. Lewis, and Charles Williams." *Mythlore* 20:4 (1995): 364-366. Print.

Howard, Thomas. *The Novels of Charles Williams*. San Francisco: Ignatius Press, 1991. Print.

Howe, Ellic. *The Magicians of the Golden Dawn: A Documentary History of a Magical Order, 1887-1923*. London: Routledge & Kegan Paul Books, 1972. Print.

Jacobs, Alan. *The Narnian: The Life and Imagination of C. S. Lewis*. New York: HarperOne, 2008. Print.

Jones, John D. Introduction. *The Divine Names and Mystical Theology*. By Pseudo-Dionysius Areopagite. Milwaukee, WI: Marquette University Press, 1980. Print.

Knight, Gareth. *The Magical World of the Inklings*. 2nd ed. Cheltenham, UK: Skylight Press, 2010. Print.

Lang-Sims, Lois. *Letters to Lalage: The Letters of Charles Williams to Lois Lang-Sims*. Kent State UP, 1989. Print.

Lewis, C. S. *English Literature in the Sixteenth Century: Excluding Drama* (Oxford History of English Literature Series). 1st ed. Oxford UP, 1954. Print.

---, Introduction. *Essays Presented to Charles Williams*. Grand Rapids, MI: Eerdmans, 1966. Print.

---, *The Collected Letters of C. S. Lewis*, ed. by Walter Hooper, 3 vols. (San Francisco, 2004-2007),

---, "On Stories." *On Stories: And Other Essays on Literature*. 1966. New York: Harcourt, 1982. 3-20. Print.

---, *The Pilgrim's Regress: An Allegorical Apology for Christianity, Reason, and Romanticism*. 1933. Grand Rapids: Eerdmans, 2001. Print.

---, *Surprised by Joy: The Shape of My Early Life*. New York: Harcourt, Brace, & Co, 1955. Print.

---, "Williams and the Arthuriad." *Taliessin through Logres; The Region of the Summer Stars*; Arthurian Torso. Grand Rapids, MI: Eerdmans, 1974. 275-384. Print.

---, "Myth Became Fact." *God in the Dock: Essays on Theology and Ethics*. 1970. Grand Rapids: Eerdmans, 2001. 63-67. Print.

Lindop, Grevel. "Re: Arthurian Commonplace Book." Message to Sørina Higgins. 27 June 2012. E-mail.

---, *Charles Williams: The Last Magician*. Unpublished.

---, "Re: 'Chapel of the Thorn' draft introductory essay." Message to Sørina Higgins. 3 April 2014. E-mail.

Loewenstein, Andrea Freud. *Loathsome Jews and Engulfing Women: Metaphors of Projection in the Works of Wyndham Lewis, Charles Williams, and Graham Greene*. New York UP, 1993. Print.

McBride, Sam, and Candice Fredrick. *Women Among the Inklings: Gender, C. S. Lewis, J. R. R. Tolkien, and Charles Williams*. Westport, CT: Praeger, 2001. Print.

McClatchey, Joe. "The Diagrammatised Glory of Charles Williams's *Taliessin*." *VII: An Anglo-American Literary Review* 2 (1981): 100-125. Print.

Mendelson, Edward. *Later Auden*. New York: Farrar, Straus and Giroux, 2000. Print.

Meynell, Alice. Letter to Charles Williams. 10 July 1914. MS. Marion E. Wade Center.

Moorman, Charles. *Arthurian Triptych: Mythic Materials in Charles Williams, C. S. Lewis, and T. S. Eliot*. Oakland, CA: University of California Press, 1960. Print.

Morrisson, Mark. *Modern Alchemy: Occultism and the Emergence of Atomic Theory*. Oxford UP, 2007. Print.
Moser, Fernando de Mello. *Charles Williams: Demanda, Visão e Mito*. Lisboa: Gráfica Santelmo, 1969. Print.
Myers, D. T. "Brave New World: The Status of Women According to Tolkien, Lewis and Williams." *Cimmaron Review* 17 (1971): 13-19. Print.
Newman, Barbara. "Charles Williams and the Companions of the Co-inherence." *Spiritus: A Journal of Christian Spirituality* 9.1 (2009): 1-26. *Project Muse*. Web. 5 June 2014.
Nyman, Amy. "Feminist Perspective in Williams' Novels." *Mythlore* 12.4 (1986): 3-9. Print.
Ridler, Anne, ed. and intro. *The Image of the City*. 1958. Berkeley, CA: Apocryphile, 2007. Print.
Ruskin, John. *The Works*. Vol. 35. Ed. E. T. Cook and Alexander Wedderburn. London: George Allen, 1903-1912. Print.
Shuttleworth, Thelma. A talk given to the Charles Williams Society at the London Conference in September 1982. Reprinted in *The Charles Williams Society Newsletter* 27 (1982): 2-7. The Charles Williams Society. Web. 4 June 2014. pdf.
Squire, Charles. *Celtic Myth and Legend: Poetry and Romance*. London: Forgotten Books, 2007. Print.
Sturch, Richard. "Charles Williams as Heretic?" *Charles Williams Quarterly* 136 (2010): 7-19. Print.
Tolkien, J. R. R. "On Fairy-Stories." *Essays Presented to Charles Williams*. Grand Rapids, MI: Eerdmans, 1966. Print. 38-89.
Waite, A. E. *Hidden Church of the Holy Graal: Its Legends and Symbolism Considered in Their Affinity with Certain Mysteries of Initiation and Other Traces of a Secret Tradition in Christian Times*. London: Rebman,1909. *Sacred-Texts.com*. Web. 5 June 2014.
---, *The Mysteries of Magic: A Digest of the Writings of Eliphas Levi*. 1886. Whitefish, MT: Kessinger Publishing, 2010. Print.
Wall, J. Charles. *Relics of the Passion*. Whitefish, MT: Kessinger Publishing, 2008. Print.
Ward, Michael. *Planet Narnia: The Seven Heavens in the Imagination of C. S. Lewis*. NY: Oxford University Press, 2008. Print.
Williams, Charles. *All Hallows' Eve*. 1945. Vancouver: Regent College Publishing, 2003. Print.
---, *Arthurian Commonplace Book*. MS. Eng. e. 2012. Bodleian Library, Oxford.
---, *The Chapel of the Thorn*. 1912. Wade CW / MS – 39. The Marion E. Wade Center, Wheaton, IL.
---. *Descent into Hell*. 1937. Grand Rapids: Eerdmans, 1980. Print.
---, *The Descent of the Dove: A Short History of the Holy Spirit in the Church*. 1939. Vancouver: Regent College Publishing, 2002. Print.
---, *The Detective Fiction Reviews of Charles Williams*, 1930-1935. Ed. Jared Lobdell. Jefferson, NC: McFarland, 2003.
---, *Divorce*. 1920. Reprints from the University of Michigan Library. Print.
---, *The English Poetic Mind*. 1932. New York: Russell & Russell, 1963. Print.
---, "Et in Sempiternum Pereant." *The London Mercury,* 1935. *Project Gutenberg Australia*. August 2008. Web. 24 July 2013.
---, *The Figure of Beatrice: A Study in Dante*. 1944. Cambridge: D. S. Brewer, 1994. Print.
---, *He Came Down from Heaven* and *Forgiveness of Sins*. 1938, 1942. Berkeley, CA: Apocryphile, 2005. Print.
---, *The House of the Octopus*. 1945. *Collected Plays*. Vancouver: Regent College Publishing, 2005. 325-374. Print.
---, *The Image of the City*. Ed. Anne Ridler. 1958. Berkeley, CA: Apocryphile, 2007. Print.
---, Letter to Alice Meynell, 6 November 1911. MS. Meynell Archive. Greatham.
---. *Many Dimensions*. 1931. Grand Rapids: Eerdmans, 1993. Print.
---, *The Masques of Amen House*. Altadena, CA: The Mythopoeic Press, 2000. Print.
---, *A Myth of Shakespeare*. 1928. Berkeley, CA: Apocryphile, 2010. Print.

---, *Outlines of Romantic Theology; with which is reprinted, Religion and love in Dante: the theology of romantic love*. Grand Rapids: Eerdmans, 1990. Print.
---, *The Place of the Lion*. 1933. Grand Rapids, MI: Eerdmans, 1980.
---, *Poems of Conformity*. 1917. *Internet Archive*. Web. 5 June 2014.
---, *Poetry at Present*. 1930. Berkeley, CA: Apocryphile, 2008. Print.
---, *Reason and Beauty in the Poetic Mind*. 1933. Eugene, OR: Wipf and Stock, 2008. Print.
---, *Seed of Adam: A Nativity Play*. 1937. *Collected Plays*. Vancouver: Regent College Publishing, 2005. 149-175. Print.
---, *Shadows of Ecstasy*. 1933. Vancouver: Regent College, 2003. Print.
---, *The Silver Stair*. London: Herbert and Daniel, 1912. Print.
---, *Thomas Cranmer of Canterbury*. 1936. *Collected Plays*. Vancouver: Regent College Publishing, 2006. 1-59. Print.
---, *Three Plays: The Early Metaphysical Plays of Charles Williams*. 1931. Eugene, OR: Wipf and Stock, 2009. Print.
---, *War in Heaven*. 1930. Grand Rapids: Eerdmans, 2004. Print.
---, *Windows of Night*. 1925. Berkeley, CA: The Apocryphile Press, 2007. Print.
Williams, Charles, and C. S. Lewis. *Taliessin through Logres; The Region of the Summer Stars; Arthurian Torso*. Grand Rapids, MI: Eerdmans, 1974. Print.

About the Author

Charles Walter Stansby Williams (1886-1945) was a British poet, novelist, literary critic, editor, teacher, biographer, Anglican Christian, and occult master. He was educated at the Abbey National School, St. Albans Grammar School, and University College London (he left without taking a degree, for financial reasons). In 1908 he began his life-long career at the Oxford University Press and also met Florence Conway; they married on April 12th, 1917. That same year, he joined The Fellowship of the Rosy Cross. Later he founded his own unofficial Order: "the Companions of the Coinherence." Williams's only child, Michael, was born in 1922. In 1924, Phyllis Jones joined the staff of the Oxford University Press in London as librarian; Williams idealized her in his Theology of Romantic Love. He gave evening lectures through the City Literary Institute until 1939, when the Press evacuated to Oxford to escape the bombing of London. There he joined "the Inklings." Oxford University invited him to lecture on Milton's *Comus* on January 20th, 1940, after which he gave tutorials and lectures and was awarded an honorary M. A. on February 18th, 1943. Williams died unexpectedly of intussusception on May 15th, 1945, just a week after victory in Europe ended England's involvement in World War II.

Williams's writing is varied, including his professional work: editing books; compiling anthologies; and writing introductions, reviews, biographies, and literary criticism (*Poetry at Present*, 1930; *The English Poetic Mind*, 1932; *Reason and Beauty in the Poetic Mind*, 1933; and *The Figure of Beatrice*, 1943). One important project was the supervision of the first English publications of Kierkegaard's works. He may have been the first person in England to lecture on Kierkegaard. He also wrote theology (*He Came Down from Heaven*, 1938; *The Forgiveness of Sins*, 1942; and *Outlines of Romantic Theology*, 1990), plays (including *The Masques of Amen House*, 1927-30; *A Myth of Shakespeare*, 1928; *Thomas Cranmer of Canterbury*, 1936; and *The House of the Octopus*, 1945), and one short story ("Et in Sempiternum Pereant," 1935).

Williams's most popular works are his seven metaphysical thriller novels: *War in Heaven* (1930), *Many Dimensions* (1931), *The Place of the Lion* (1931), *The Greater Trumps* (1932), *Shadows of Ecstasy* (1933), *Descent into Hell* (1937), and *All Hallow's Eve* (1945). His two volumes of Arthurian poetry are his masterpiece: *Taliessin through Logres* (1938) and *The Region of the Summer Stars* (1944). The novels and Arthurian poetry place him among the literary masters of the early 20th century.

About the Editor

Sørina Higgins (www.sorinahiggins.com) is a writer, editor, English teacher, Inklings scholar, and author of the blog *The Oddest Inkling*, devoted to a systematic study of Charles Williams's works. Visit it at http://TheOddestInkling.wordpress.com/. She is available to speak, teach, and write about the Inklings, poetry, or the arts and faith. Please follow @Oddest_Inkling and @SorinaHiggins on twitter.

Higgins is currently editing an essay collection entitled *The Inklings and King Arthur* that examines Tolkien's *The Fall of Arthur* in the context of other Arthurian works by his contemporaries, including Williams. She is Book, Film, and Play Review Editor of *Sehnsucht: The C. S. Lewis Journal*. Her article entitled "Double Affirmation: Medievalism as Christian Apologetic in the Arthurian Poetry of Charles Williams" is included in a topical issue of *The Journal of Inklings Studies* (October 2013), and a chapter called "Is a 'Christian' Mystery Story Possible? Charles Williams' War in Heaven as a Generic Case Study" appears in *Christianity & the Detective Story* (Cambridge Scholars, 2013).

Higgins holds an M.A. from Middlebury College's Bread Loaf School of English. She serves as a Preceptor at Signum University and teaches English at Lehigh Carbon Community College. She hosts Ekphrasis: Fellowship of Christians in the Arts, a monthly workshop-and-critique group in Eastern Pennsylvania. She has published two volumes of poetry, *The Significance of Swans* and *Caduceus*. Like everybody else, she is writing her first novel. Sørina and her husband designed and built their own house, without experience or expertize, and it hasn't fallen down around them yet.